The Death Boat

The tragic accident on West Lake Okoboji that left nine
dead and changed boating in Iowa forever

Lloyd B. Cunningham

Copyright © by Lloyd B. Cunningham, 2019

All rights reserved. No part of this book may be reproduced in any form by an electronic or mechanical means, including information storage and retrieval systems, without permission in writing from the publisher, except by a reviewer who may quote brief passages in a review.

ISBN: 9781795084796

Cover by Kristy Anderson

Images courtesy of the
Iowa Great Lakes Maritime Museum &
The Spencer Daily Reporter

☆☆☆

To my wife Linda,
for her support, encouragement and patience,
and to the nine passengers who lost their lives in the sinking of *Miss Thriller*

CONTENTS

Preface	1
Prologue	5
Chapter One: Albert Hickman's New Boat	11
Chapter Two: West Lake Okoboji and Arnolds Park	21
Chapter Three: The Launching of *Miss Thriller*	31
Chapter Four: *Miss Thriller* Moves to Okoboji	37
Chapter Five: Boat Line Warfare	49
Chapter Six: The Day of the Accident	57
Chapter Seven: Recovery of the Bodies	71
Chapter Eight: The Funerals	73
Chapter Nine: News Coverage of the Accident	77
Chapter Ten: Governor Hammill Steps In	93
Chapter Eleven: Recovery of *Miss Thriller*	105
Chapter Twelve: Epilogue	115
Acknowledgements	125

Preface

I stumbled across the story of *Miss Thriller* as I was assembling a different book, a collection of my underwater photographs from West Lake Okoboji in northwest Iowa. While researching the stories behind the boats that still lie on the bottom of the lake, it occurred to me that an important part of my book should answer the question: Who was the first diver in Lake Okoboji?

My first stop was the Iowa Great Lakes Maritime Museum in Arnolds Park. From previous visits, I knew the museum had a display of artifacts collected by early scuba divers and perhaps, I hoped, it would have a history of diving in the lake. The scuba display contained little history, but a mannequin in a diving suit across the museum caught my eye. It was part of a display about a boating accident that took nine lives in 1929 when two passenger boats, *Miss Thriller* and *Zipper,* collided in the dark in the middle of the lake. *Miss Thriller,* reported to be the fastest boat ever to race across West Okoboji, sank to the bottom of the lake. Newspaper accounts with the exhibit said a hard-hat diver, Captain Thompson of Duluth, Minnesota, was brought to the Lakes the following summer to recover *Miss Thriller* and salvage the airplane engines that made her so fast.

I contacted officials at the Lake Superior Maritime Museum in Duluth to see if they knew of a Captain Thompson. They did, and they put me in touch with his granddaughter Marie Thompson Norick. She was happy to share stories about her grandfather, Captain Horace Herbert Thompson, and his son John, who also became a diver. Marie tendered for John, her dad, before she tendered for, and later married, yet another hard-hat diver, Jerry Norick. Marie sent me copies of the family's diving stories, newspaper clippings about Captain Thompson's dives at Okoboji, and a few photographs. It seemed evident that Thompson was the first diver in the lake, and now that I had a part of the story, I couldn't put it down. I needed to know everything I could about *Miss Thriller*, from the design of her high-performance hull to her launching, sinking, salvage, and eventual destruction.

The research took me on a journey through court records and transcripts, historic newspapers and magazines, and history books on Iowa and Dickinson County. I traveled to libraries across the state and contacted libraries and museums from Pictou, Nova Scotia, Canada, to Seattle, Washington. I sorted through U.S. Census records, antique travel brochures, period bulletins, and private correspondence. I conducted hundreds of Internet searches, piecing together the story of what newspapers of the period called the "Fastest Boat On Earth."[1]

What I learned is that the story of *Miss Thriller* is really a story about the people whose lives were changed by the boat. To tell that story, I needed to know who they were, and I began with her victims. I knew almost immediately their names needed to be verified. Spellings varied with almost every newspaper that printed the list. Checking them against the official records ultimately required me to make some decisions. The birth certificate for the crash's youngest victim spells his name as Neal Gelino. On his death certificate, it lists the 11-year-old as Neil Gelino. I chose to use the spelling on his birth certificate, and I was forced to make similar decisions with other people in the story.

The first part of the twentieth century was also an era when men, and newspapers that wrote about them, identified themselves by their initials. Women were simply identified by their last name. C.P. Benit, Dr. A.L. Peck, Dr. P.G. Grimm, Judge C.P. Price, Captain W.E.G. Saunders, Mrs. Hintz, Mrs. Gelino, and Mrs. Addy all are important to the story, but what were their full names? A cadre of genealogists, most of whom I know only by their email signatures, helped me uncover them. With their full names, I

---

[1] "Fastest Boat On Earth," *Milford (Iowa) Mail*, Thursday, May 14, 1925: 1
[2] Roderick A. Smith, *A History of Dickinson County, Iowa: Together with an account of The Spirit*

learned more about who they were and what part they played in the story. I used their first name on their first reference in every case except that of Saunders.

For years, I assumed that one of three men to be put on trial after the accident spelled his name Harold Yarnes. Almost every newspaper and almost all arrest records, indictments and court documents spelled it that way. Even the newspaper reporter who interviewed the pilot and wrote his only firsthand account 60 years after the accident spelled his last name with an E. It wasn't until I found his signature on a letter to Iowa's governor asking that his pilot's license be returned that I discovered his name was spelled Yarns. That's also the spelling on his headstone in the Lakeview Cemetery in Spirit Lake, Iowa.

Assembling the history of the boat was almost as difficult as identifying the people in the story. *Miss Thriller's* inventor, William Albert Hickman, never used his first name. James Claude Ellis, her first owner, used several stage and professional names. Charles Parker, who brought the boat to West Lake Okoboji, shared his name with other Charles Parkers living in the area. Complicated business arrangements obscured her ownership after Parker sold the launch, but eventually I was able to put together a complete history of the boat and then weave together the people and the boat into this tragic yet, I think, very interesting story.

Today, almost 90 years after *Miss Thriller* sank in West Lake Okoboji, several versions of how and why the crash occurred remain, and opinions differ about who was responsible for the accident. Out of respect for her victims, those who lived through the events of 1924-34, their descendants, and the people who live at the Lakes today, I have tried to be as accurate as possible telling their story. It has been my pleasure to write, and I hope readers enjoy it.

The Death Boat

Prologue

West Lake Okoboji, a remarkably clear, blue-water lake in northwest Iowa, has always beckoned people to her shores. Traders and trappers were drawn to her bountiful fishing and hunting. Settlers came for the rich black soil, forested hills, and drinkable water. Visitors and travelers still come to play in her waters, rest on her sandy beaches, and enjoy her beautiful scenery. She is the home of leisurely summer afternoons and romantic sunsets, the kind of place where visitors, as early as the 1880s, left with sweet memories and bottles of beach sand to show their friends.

By 1920, she was also the home to Arnolds Park, the famous summer resort community wrapped around Pillsbury Point on the south shore of Cass Bay. Every summer, her full-time population of almost 500 grew to more than 10,000 residents, while her amusement parks hosted 100,000 tourists and travelers from across the Midwest and from as far away as both coasts.

Gone and almost forgotten were the Native Americans, who in 1857 had killed the original settlers around the lake and carried off four young women, one just 14 years old. A relief expedition from Fort Dodge, 100 miles away, arrived too late to spare the settlers; all they could do was bury the dead. Two members of the expedition froze to death in the rescue attempt as they battled waist-deep snow, a blinding blizzard, and temperatures plunging to 38 degrees below zero. Almost 40 years later, a 55-foot-high monument to the settlers and the relief expedition was erected on the site where the first victims died. Made of alternating sections of rough and polished Minnesota granite, it stands on Pillsbury Point near the center of Arnolds Park and overlooks the beach and its famous amusement park.

Gone was her fleet of steamboats, powered at first by wood and later by coal. They began appearing in the early 1880s. They carried visitors, arriving on horse-drawn wagons and passenger trains at the place then known as Arnold's park, across the lake to the early fishing camps and budding resort hotels that roads had yet to reach. The steamers numbered almost a dozen at the turn of the century. They carried as many as 300 passengers and their luggage on regularly scheduled routes around West Lake Okoboji and to the towns of Spirit Lake and Orleans on adjoining East Lake Okoboji.

Gone too was Wesley B. Arnold, who established the community that bears his name. Arnold moved his family onto the hill overlooking the beach in 1864. By then, the area was already a well-known campground for hunters and fishermen. His front yard became, in the words of historian Roderick A. Smith, "storm center,"[2] the very crossroads of the railroads bringing travelers to the lake and the steamboats that carried them across her waters. Arnold began supplying whatever his visitors required. In 1882, he built a house with a large kitchen from which to feed them. Later, he built a hotel and a pavilion where they could hold their meetings, church gatherings, and political speeches.

In 1889, he built what became the very beginning of his famous amusement park: a toboggan slide. It was a wooden chute with steel rollers on the bottom built 60 feet high at the water's edge. It sloped steeply down to the lake and then stretched out over shallow water. Bathers carried sleds to the top, climbed onboard, and rode down the chute with a rumble. The sleds shot off the end of the slide and skipped across the water until they settled in the lake with a splash. The ride was eventually called Shoot the Chute.

In February 1897, the residents at Arnold's park petitioned the District Court for permission to incorporate their growing community. The court

---

[2] Roderick A. Smith, *A History of Dickinson County, Iowa: Together with an account of The Spirit Lake Massacre, and the Indian Troubles on the Northwestern Frontier.* The Kenyon Printing & Mfg. Co., Des Moines, 1902: 528

granted the request and appointed a commission to set an election date. On March 30, 1897, 50 votes were cast, 31 for and 19 against, and Arnold's park became the town of Arnolds Park. Wesley B. Arnold was elected to the first city council.

The 1920s were good to Americans. It was a decade of unprecedented prosperity. Women gained the right to vote and real wages improved, generating more disposable income for the purchase of consumer goods. Businesses and manufacturing industries were continuously expanding and turning out furniture, ready-to-wear clothing, and processed foods. Families were buying electric devices such as washing machines and vacuum cleaners, and every day more Americans were buying radios. Henry Ford's assembly-line production methods put the Model-T within reach of the average family, and travel expanded across the country on improving roads and highways. Telephone service was working its way across the country and around the Iowa Great Lakes. Farm prices, badly depressed by post-war production surpluses, had taken almost 10 years to recover, but even those who made their living farming enjoyed remarkably stable prices after the middle of the decade and could find time and money for entertainment.

Arnolds Park expanded with the country. By 1929, it was the home of a pair of impressive amusement parks. Between them, they had the largest roller coaster, the largest roller-skating rink, and the largest dance floor in Iowa. The parks offered carnival rides and games, a funhouse, and a moving picture theatre. Along the waterfront were a grocery, a barbershop, and souvenir stands. Popular refreshments and complete meals were available from walk-up booths and at a sit-down restaurant. Visitors could rent fishing gear, and rowing and sailing boats from the beach. They also could board one of the three remaining steamboats, the *Queen*, *Des Moines* or *Sioux City*, at the Okoboji Steamboat Company dock in front of the Benit Amusement Park. Each offered tours and passage to the dance pavilions at the resort hotels around the lake.

In an era when private boat ownership was rare, speedboats were among the most popular attractions at Arnolds Park. Several operators offered speedboat rides from docks in front of Peck's Amusement Park. Some offered leisure tours along the lakeshore and across the bay. Others offered thrilling, high-speed rides promising a chance to get wet from the splash and spray. There always seemed to be lines of people waiting to ride the speedboats. Two competing operators claimed to have the fastest boat on the lake, and they challenged one another for every rider who came to the beach.

Sunday night, July 28, 1929, the amusement parks and the waterfront were packed with thousands of visitors seeking relief from the summer's heat and looking for a good time. Sundays always drew the largest crowds; it was the age of the six-day workweek, and almost everyone had the day off. The music of the orchestra playing on the second-floor Roof Garden Ballroom drifted out its opened windows and down to the street. There it mixed with the sounds of carnival machinery, midway barkers, and the mechanical tunes of the carousel on the beach. From inside the parks came the screams of delight from the riders aboard the roller coasters and swing rides.

About 9:40 p.m., a motorboat from across the lake, the 20-passenger *Reliance*, rushed toward the beach and landed at the Eagle Boat Line docks. Her pilot, Frank Hopkins, and his passengers were calling out for help. Sprawled across the boat's seats were six soaking-wet and visibly shaken survivors from the motorboat *Miss Thriller*, a 16-passenger launch that offered high-speed boat rides from the docks in front of the amusement parks. *Miss Thriller* had been hit in the dark and sunk by another passenger boat one-half mile south of Dixon Beach. Hopkins and his passengers, who had heard the crash and responded to the screams for help, rushed to the scene and pulled everyone they could find out of the water.

The survivors were *Miss Thriller's* pilot and co-pilot Frank Long and Jasper "Jap" Alexander; Guy Hedrick, a local sign painter; two schoolboys, Kenneth Darlington and Roy Barnes; and a bookkeeper from Des Moines, Lucille Patterson. The questions of where the rest of *Miss Thriller's* passengers were, who had hit the boat and what had happened to its pilot and passengers would slowly begin to unfold as other survivors were brought to shore in what became the deadliest boating accident in Iowa.

Over the course of the next four years, a coroner's inquest and a grand jury investigation would be conducted. Men would be charged with second-degree murder, manslaughter and conspiracy. Families who lost loved ones would file civil lawsuits. The governor would ban passenger boats from operating after dark, and the state conservation board would adopt stringent rules governing the operation of all motorboats on Iowa lakes. Four trials would take place, and a pilot would be sentenced to prison. Eventually, decisions would be handed down by Iowa's 14th District Court and the Iowa and Minnesota supreme courts. The accident on that final Sunday night in July 1929 would take the lives of nine people and change boating in Iowa forever.

The Death Boat

Chapter One

Albert Hickman's New Boat

On August 21, 1922, the *Daily Times* of Watertown, New York, sent a reporter to the small village of Alexandria Bay, an hour north by automobile. His assignment: to witness the launching of a new high-speed powerboat. Such an attraction would be an important addition to the Thousand Islands, a popular tourist destination for the rich and famous, located on the banks of the St. Lawrence River. Gar Wood, a widely respected designer, builder and racer of powerboats, and holder of the water speed record at the time of 71.43 miles an hour, had predicted this new launch—a passenger boat—could reach speeds of 75 miles an hour.

The reporter, working his way through hundreds of curious onlookers and the long line of passengers along the Cornwell Brothers' dock eager to ride the boat, might have been surprised by what he saw. Not a line or feature of this new launch suggested it was built for speed. The boat looked like a small barge, a 30-foot-by-8-foot wooden box with square ends and flat sides. The box's front was wider than its rear. Cut into the top were two compartments. The larger compartment, near the bow, held four bench seats, four passengers to a bench. The rear compartment held a pair of 300-horsepower Fiat airplane engines mounted side by side. Each had a short drive shaft and drove a propeller that stuck out the back of the boat rather than out its bottom. Only the lower half of the propellers reached into the water. The engine compartment had places for two hands, a pilot and a mechanic/lookout. The latter threw the engines in and out of gear.

The Death Boat

The pilot used a pair of throttles to steer the launch. Pushed forward together, they drove the boat straight ahead; pushed forward independently, they turned the boat left or right. A small steering device controlled odd-looking plates mounted on the sides of the boat near the stern. They were used to steer the craft at slow speeds and in tight quarters. The launch could not be driven in reverse.

With every seat filled, the pilot eased the boat away from the dock and into the river, where he engaged the throttles. The propellers shot a plume of white water high into the air until they got a bite on the water and then the boat rose to the surface and raced across the river on a cushion of water spray and air generated by the shape of its bottom. The pilot made a loop out into the channel around Sunken Rock Lighthouse and back at a speed that seemed impossible for such a boxy-looking craft. The engines' roar could be heard four miles away.

Over the next 11 years, the boat would be known as the most popular attraction on the St. Lawrence River, the fastest passenger launch in the country, and a government-built submarine chaser. Later, detractors would accuse her of being unseaworthy, and eventually newspapers would refer to her as the Death Boat. But that Monday morning as her thrilled and giggling passengers stumbled out of the launch and onto the boardwalk at the end of Market Street, they told the reporter the boat certainly had been aptly named. She was called *Miss Thriller*.

Miss Thriller was a sea sled, a high-performance motor launch whose hull design, surface-piercing propellers, and unique steering systems allowed her to achieve very high speeds, perhaps as fast as 70 miles an hour, by skimming across the water's surface on a cushion of water spray and air.

Sea sleds were the creation of Canadian William Albert Hickman. Hickman, who never used his first name, was born into a wealthy shipbuilding family in December 1878. He grew up in Pictou, Nova Scotia, an outdoorsman who enjoyed hunting and fishing. He was a sculler at Harvard University, where in 1899 he graduated with a degree in marine engineering. After graduation, Hickman was appointed Commissioner for New Brunswick, a government position that took him to Great Britain. There, he lectured extensively about the Province of New Brunswick and Canada's abundant business and development opportunities.

On his return, he traveled and wrote about New Brunswick's agriculture, resources, and industries. At the same time, he wrote the best-selling romantic adventure novel "The Sacrifice of the Shannon." All the while, Hickman was tinkering with an idea for a hull design that would provide "the greatest available speed with the least available power."[3]

In 1907, he put his ideas into wood, building a 20-foot scow of tongue-and-grooved spruce flooring. The boat had a flat bottom and flat sides and looked, he said, "not unlike an inexpensive coffin for a very large person, carried to a point at one end."[4] He called the boat *Viper*, and according to Hickman, she easily outran other boats of the same horsepower. The principles of his design, he later wrote, were "so simple that it seems ridiculous to say they have not all been tried in one hull before."[5] With *Viper II*, Hickman tested engine positions and propeller shaft angles, looking for a way to reduce the pounding created by the boat's flat bottom. In 1910, with the precise placements found, Hickman built *Viper III*, published his design, and wrote extensively about its performance. His ideas were a direct affront to traditional designs that called for V-bottomed and round-sided boats.

Critics widely attacked his boat. They questioned his basic understanding of marine engineering and his testing methods and suggested he must have run his trials on some small, obscure Canadian lake where they wouldn't be seen and questioned. Seth G. Malby, a widely respected marine writer and author of "The Resistance of Power Boats and a Method of Measuring Same," suggested that his tests were "run with the aid of an alarm clock over 'we-call-it-a-mile length' and [with a] speed indicator which was borrowed from the village mechanic."[6] In fact, Hickman's trials were conducted on busy Pictou Harbor over a carefully measured distance and timed with precision maritime instruments.

But Hickman's boat had fans as well as detractors. *Vipers* were built around the world, and proponents found them to be fast and fun. The Bath Marine Construction Company of Maine, one of the first commercial firms to build

---

[3] Albert Hickman, "How To Build A Viper," The Rudder Publishing Company, NY, 1911: 7
[4] Albert Hickman, "The Sea Sled," *The American Magazine*, July 1914: 44
[5] W. Albert Hickman, "The Viper Type of Speed Boat," *The Rudder*, April 1910: 346
[6] Seth G. Malby, "Weary of Practice," *The Rudder*, May 1910: 406

a *Viper*, said, "No cheaper, faster or safer boat was ever devised by man."[7] In solid support for the flat-bottomed boat, Lyman J. Seely, president of Elbridge Engine Company and owner of a *Viper*, wrote in *Rudder* magazine in January 1911, "Mr. Hickman is dead right in the matter…for *Viper* is the fastest and most seaworthy boat on record, at the price."[8]

While the debate on *Viper III's* shape and performance went on in boating magazines, Hickman continued to modify his design. An inspired observer, he saw wasted energy in the spray the *Viper's* flat bottom threw out to the sides. To capture that energy, he added blades that extended into the water on the sides of his boat. The blades trapped the spray beneath the boat, so it rode on a cushion of water spray and air, allowing it to run much faster with the same power.

The test convinced Hickman that the fastest way to run a boat wasn't to plow it through the water but to skim it across the surface. He began testing hull shapes that would create the water spray and air cushion and started looking for a way to drive and steer the boat from above the water's surface. Two *Vipers* later, he had achieved both. In February 1913, Hickman applied for patents and took his final design, *Viper V*, to the New York International Motor Boat Show at Madison Square Garden.

Full naval ceremonies opened the 1913 New York International Motor Boat Show. It was the first time the U.S. Navy had taken an official interest in the boat show. Secretary of the Navy George von L. Meyer, with an eye on deteriorating political developments in Europe, was struggling with the U.S. Congress to maintain the Navy's strength and readiness in an era of isolationism and neutrality. He hoped to use the motorboat show to enhance the public's view of the Navy and boost his funding. His officers were eager to thoroughly inspect the latest developments in marine gasoline engines and their application in torpedo boats.

When the doors opened at 3 p.m. February 15, 1913, a capacity crowd filled the amphitheater to see ceremonies the Navy usually saved for a warship's commissioning. As Secretary Meyer and assisting naval officers arrived at the Garden, an honor guard of 135 sailors in full military dress, standing in

---

[7] Bath Marine Construction Company, "Viper II (magazine ad)," *The Rudder*, June 1910: 54
[8] Lyman J. Seely, "More Viper," *The Rudder*, April 1911: 324

a double line along the sidewalk, snapped to attention. The group passed through the line to the foyer, where a chief boatswain's mate piped order on a shrill whistle. Eight sideboys, ceremonial assistants to the secretary, saluted crisply as a drum and bugle corps played "Ruffles and Flourishes." The crowd inside, hearing the fanfare and seeing Meyer in the doorway, let out a roaring cheer.

A huge gun inside the amphitheater boomed a 19-round welcome, and Secretary Meyer proceeded to the platform. In brief remarks, he declared the show open. With that, a large American flag, which had been furled up in a building girder, fell gracefully through the air while the band played "The Star-Spangled Banner." Everyone in the Garden saluted. After the ceremonies, Secretary Meyer and his staff walked through the exhibits and congratulated the management on a fine show. Navy officials shuffled in and out of the Garden, inspecting the displays and gathering information. One of the exhibits that drew their special attention was Albert Hickman's *Viper V*.

Hickman's new boat was completely unexpected. In addition to its uncommon boxy shape, it had a V-shaped tunnel down the hull's center, deep at the bow and shallowing to a flat bottom at the stern. Its cross-section resembled the letter W. The launch was driven by a pair of surface-piercing propellers that reached down into the water from the back of the boat and turned in opposite directions to compensate for the sideways torque each generated. In open water, the steering was done by varying the speed of the engines. More throttle to the left engine turned the boat to the right; more right throttle turned the boat left. At slow speeds, steering was accomplished by brass plates that were attached with hinges on their forward edges on the sides of the boat near the stern. Operated independently by a small wheel near the pilot, rods on the back of the boat pushed out the left plate to turn left or the right plate to turn right. When underway, the V-shaped tunnel scooped water spray and air under the boat, lifting it high enough to skim across the surface of the water.

Boat-show officials snubbed Hickman and his *Viper*. They relegated it to the basement beneath the main showroom floor, and his name and boat were left off the official list of exhibitors printed in the *New York Herald*. The yachting world was stunned after seeing the boat. Her shape offended their sense of what a gentleman's launch should look like. Some called the boat "a squat and ugly craft,"[9] while others said she was "awkward-looking."[10] Kinder observers said simply it was "not a handsome launch,"[11] but most of Hickman's earlier critics were silent. They didn't know how to respond to a boat of its shape.

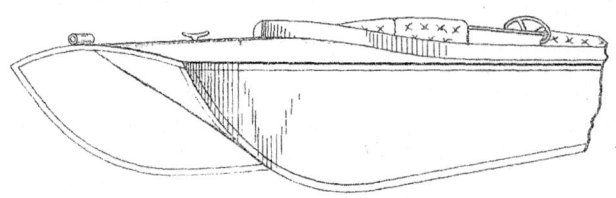

Hickman's Sea Sled
From U.S. Patent No. 1,204,355 issued to W.A. Hickman, November 7, 1916

Charles Chapman, editor of *MotorBoating* magazine, inspected *Viper V* at the show and wrote, "Any resemblance to a boat could not be recognized."[12] Worst of all for those offended by its looks, the boat did all the things Hickman said it would. It planed faster, it needed less power to achieve the same speeds as conventional hulls, it was a drier ride because all the spray went under the boat, it could run in shallower water than other launches because of the propeller placement, it was more stable in rough seas, and it was faster than any other hull on the water. Hickman called his design an inverted V-bottom, but "the ship gave so perfectly the impression of a sled running on ice," he said, "she was nicknamed sea sled."[13] It became the name of the whole new class of boats.

While the yachting world turned up its collective nose at the boat, many boating writers noticed and loved the sea sled, especially because she performed exactly as advertised. Hickman was delighted with the reception. He opened an office in Boston and began a relationship with experienced boat builders Murray & Tregurtha Company to construct his sea sleds. Every sea sled from 1913 until 1919 was built in its Boston boatyard.

---

[9] "War Notes" *The Nelson (New Zealand) Evening Mail*, Friday April 13, 1917: 4
[10] "Fourth World's Record Broken By Speed Boats," *Buffalo (NY) Evening News*, Monday, August 15, 1921: 17
[11] *Journal of the Military Service Institution of the United States*, Volume 58, January-June 1916: 323
[12] Chars. F. Chapman, "Picking the American B.I.T. Boats," *MotorBoating*, August 1913: 48
[13] Albert Hickman, "The Sea Sled," *The American Magazine*, July 1914: 86

Hickman left the 1913 boat show with orders for at least three boats.

Commodore J. Stuart Blackton of the Atlantic Yacht Club purchased the first sea sled. He planned to enter it the following September in the British International Trophy Races at Osborne Bay, England. His sea sled was delivered in July, just days before the elimination races at Huntington, Long Island, New York. It was 28 feet long, had a 7-foot beam, and was powered by a pair of 8-cylinder, 180-horsepower Van Blerck engines. Blackton named her *America*, and Hickman himself drove her during the trials. Unfortunately, nagging engine problems prevented *America* from finishing the trials, so she did not qualify for the trip to England. *America*, Blackton's 14th racing boat, became his personal runabout at the family's summer home on Oyster Bay, New York.

Philanthropist Vincent Astor, son of multimillionaire John Jacob Astor who had died on the *RMS Titanic*, bought the second sea sled. He called her *Noma*. She was delivered to the New Jersey harbor near his home in August. *Noma* was 18 feet long at the water line, 5 feet at its beam. She was a five-passenger pleasure boat he often raced against friends. *Noma*, with her six-cylinder in-line engine, could reach 30 miles an hour. *The New York Times* said she looked like a "large toboggan car."[14] Other New York newspapers took to calling it the "queer looking craft"[15] when Astor was seen motoring in the harbor near his home.

Hickman's most important sale was to the Navy. Naval officials were interested in its promised performance of 36 miles an hour. The Navy ordered that a 24-foot sea sled with a pair of 75-horsepower engines be demonstrated in Boston in September. That sea sled reached the promised 36 miles an hour. Impressed, the Navy ordered two larger, 30-foot-by-11-foot sea sleds, fitted with a pair of 8-cylinder engines. They performed perfectly while reaching speeds of 43 miles per hour. The Navy, and later the Army, was so impressed by their performance that sea sleds became their exclusive high-speed boat for the duration of World War I.

Sea sleds were put into service as tenders for seaplanes and warships, ambulances, crash-and-rescue boats, and, after the United States entered the

---

[14] "Astor's New Hydroplane," *The New York Times*, Friday, August 15, 1913: 16
[15] "Vincent Astor Tries His New "Sea Sled"," *New York (NY) World*, Friday, August 15, 1913: 1

The Death Boat

war, patrol boats, some armed with one or a pair of Lewis machine guns. During World War I, war-boat building took over almost all of the sea sled building capacity at the M&T shipyards. To meet the need for sea sleds, the Navy bought privately owned sea sleds, leased others, and contacted builders around the country known to be able to craft fine wooden boats about building additional sea sleds. By September 1918, at least 60 sea sleds, stationed along the Atlantic Coast, were patrolling for German submarines.[16]

The Navy also tested torpedo-armed sea sleds for coastal defense, and the Army commissioned Hickman to build sea sleds as launching platforms for Caproni bombers. Both were successful, but the war ended before either saw service. Boats under construction, including the torpedo boats and aircraft launchers, were abandoned. While the Army continued purchasing sea sleds for coastal and inland water use through at least 1930, the Navy was selling off its sea sleds by December 1919.

When Prohibition began, the U.S. Coast Guard, which had sea sleds in its inventory as early as 1917, began buying the high-speed boats for open-water liquor law enforcement. In 1924, the Coast Guard ordered 40 35-foot cabined sea sleds for rum-running patrols. The first were delivered in August, joining the picket lines along Long Island Sound to run down bootleggers ferrying illegal liquor to shore. Others saw service on the Great Lakes and along the St. Lawrence River.

Rum-runners used sea sleds too. At least two sea sleds, running liquor from offshore into Miami, were captured, armed, and put into service by the Coast Guard in November 1926.[17] The Boeing Airplane Company may have provided other sea sleds to rum-runners. After wartime-airplane orders ended, Boeing began building sea sleds in its hangars at Seattle. The company had sold only three of 10 until a few months after Prohibition began. The remaining sea sleds were listed in a Seattle newspaper classified advertisement, and they sold the next day.[18] The rumor at the company was that the boats, paid for in cash, were sold to rum-runners.

---

[16] "Submarine-chaser in Texas," *The Yonkers (NY) Statesman,* Saturday, September 21, 1918: 1
[17] "Rum Running on East Coast Is Passing Into History," *St. Petersburg (FL) Times,* Friday, November 6, 1925: 37
[18] Gordon Newell, *Ready All: George Yeoman Pocock and Crew Racing* (University of Washington Press, 1987): 61

To further public awareness and generate sales, Hickman began building racing boats to keep his sea sleds on the pages of major newspapers. In 1921, a pair of his sea sleds, *Orlo II* and *Orlo III*, built for wealthy New York dredging contractor George Leary and his son, set speed records in every trophy series race they entered from Miami, Florida, to Detroit, Michigan. In August that year, *The New York Times* reported that *Orlo III* had shattered the speed record for displacement boats at the International Regatta in Buffalo, New York, by reaching 61.22 miles an hour, 10 miles an hour faster than the previous record. At the wheel was her designer, Albert Hickman. His advertising and exploits were so successful that by 1933 the Hickman Sea Sled Company's facilities at West Mystic, Connecticut, and later in nearby Groton, built and sold more than 6,000 sea sleds.

But Hickman's success was not to last. Sea sleds slowly fell out of fashion, partly because he was a better engineer than salesman and partly because their shape was difficult and expensive to build in wood. They were hard to frame and plank, and harder to repair. The boat was heavy for its dimensions and hard to turn, especially at slow speeds because of the resistance of the parallel keels created by the hull's tunnel. The side plate rudders were inefficient, and sea sleds were slow starters. The surface propellers churned the water into a froth, throwing up a signature rooster tail until the blades could grip the water. Perhaps most damaging was the boat's odd shape: Sea sleds just didn't have much eye appeal. However, the launch did achieve great speed with relatively little power, and as Norman L. Skene, author of "Elements of Yacht Design," wrote about Hickman's hull, "from a weight/speed standpoint the sea sled was one of the most efficient hulls ever built."[19]

---

[19] Norman L. Skene, *Elements of Yacht Design,* (Kennedy Bros, New York, 6th ed., 1938): 219

The Death Boat

Chapter Two

West Lake Okoboji and Arnolds Park

West Lake Okoboji is the centerpiece of a chain of lakes in northwest Iowa. Most lie to her east and south, and are rounded, sandy-bottomed lakes less than 25 feet deep. Big Spirit Lake, the largest natural lake in Iowa, drains across a narrow isthmus into East Lake Okoboji at the town of Orleans. Water links the rest of the chain: Upper Gar, Minnewashta, and Lower Gar. Their waters flow from north to south and empty into Milford Creek, the Little Sioux River, and eventually into the Missouri River. The waters of West Lake Okoboji join the flow at the south end of East Okoboji through a navigable channel that allows passage north to the towns of Spirit Lake on her northwest shore and Orleans at the isthmus.

West Lake Okoboji is the deepest natural lake in Iowa. The heart of the lake stretches from Terrace Park Beach in the south to Triboji Beach more than five and one-half miles to the north. In places, the lake is almost two miles wide. Left behind by the last glacier to reach deep into the Midwest 14,000 years ago, part of her shoreline is banked with large, tumbled stone. Elsewhere, she has gently sloping sandy beaches. Dense oak forests shade the rolling hills overlooking the lake. Her major bays have hard, sand-covered bottoms and vary in depth from 20 to 35 feet. In some places, aquatic plants grow 20 feet tall, almost reaching the surface in late summer. They provide nurseries for panfish and hunting grounds for walleye, northern pike, and muskie. The bottom of the lake, 138 feet at its deepest point, is layered in thick muck that can be more than 4 feet deep. Her depth, uncommon for an inland prairie lake, is responsible for her beautiful blue color. Silts, sediments and microscopic plant life quickly settle through the water near the surface, leaving it clear and able to create handsome reflections of the blue sky.

European explorers heard of the lakes in the late 1600s from the Native Americans. Explorers Meriwether Lewis and William Clark, on their Corps of Discovery Expedition from 1804 to 1806, never came closer to Okoboji than the Missouri River's turn to the northwest near what's now Sioux City, Iowa, about 110 miles away. They sketched the lakes on their map based on the descriptions from the local inhabitants. Cartographer Joseph Nicollet, who led a U.S. Army Corps of Engineers' surveying expedition to map the region between the upper Mississippi and Missouri rivers, visited the lakes in September 1838. He put Okoboji on his map by name. In 1850, Fort Clarke, later renamed Fort Dodge, was established at the junction of Des Moines River and Lizard Creek as the frontier outpost of northern Iowa, 100 miles southeast of the lakes.[20] With the signing of the Treaty of Traverse des Sioux in 1851, the last of the Native Americans gave up all claims to the land in northwest Iowa, and the area was opened for settlement.

In July 1856, a year before Dickinson County, Iowa, was organized, the first settlers arrived at the shore of West Okoboji Lake. Among them were Rowland and Frances Gardner, their children, son-in-law Harvey Luce, and two grandchildren. Rowland Gardner claimed much of the land and lakeshore around Pillsbury Point that later became the city of Arnolds Park. He built a one-room log cabin for his family on the hill above the beach. On March 7, 1857, a band of Wahpekute Sioux led by Chief Inkpaduta arrived at the Gardner cabin cold, hungry and angry that white people were living on their hunting grounds. During the next five days, the party murdered 35 to 40 homesteaders in the last Native American attack on settlers in Iowa. Fourteen-year-old Abbie Gardner watched as her family members were killed. Then, she and three other young women were taken captive. Two were subsequently killed, one released, and Abbie, the youngest, was ransomed three months later for two horses, two kegs of gunpowder, blankets, and trade goods. Chief Inkpaduta, who 19 years later

---

[20] "Fort Clarke," *The New Orleans (LA) Crescent,* Monday, October 28, 1850: 2

fought at the Battle of the Little Bighorn in what now is southeastern Montana, eventually made his way to Canada. He lived there the rest of his life. No one was ever brought to justice for what became known as the Spirit Lake Massacre.

The following spring, the Rev. John Samuel Prescott, wife Mary, and most of their seven children came to West Lake Okoboji. He bought and enlarged the Gardner claim and built a small house for his family where he set aside a room for church services. Prescott was a Methodist preacher who had founded a religious center and two churches in Fond du Lac, Wisconsin. He planned to build a religious and cultural center near Pillsbury Point, overlooking the lake. He served on the first Board of Supervisors for Dickinson County and performed the first marriage in the county at his home in 1859. He eventually abandoned his plans to build a college and left the lakes, but not before selling the Gardner claim in the fall of 1864 to another Wisconsin family, Wesley B. and Eunice Arnold and daughters Luella, Hattie, and Mabel.

By the time Prescott sold to Arnold, the grove of oak trees on the hill above the sandy beach had become a popular camping site. Most of the visitors came from easy riding distances and stayed a few days, but by the late 1870s large parties from as far away as Des Moines, Iowa, and St. Louis, Missouri, were making annual camping trips to the lake. The visitors picnicked, swam in the blue waters, fished, and played baseball along the low bank. By 1880, the area was known as Arnold's park and its owner and host Wesley Arnold, provided anything to attract and interest a crowd. He let them tent on the hills above the beach and rented out rooms in his house. He built cabins they could rent.

In 1882, he built a house with a large kitchen that he used to provide them meals. Arnold built a hotel facing the lake with what he described in *Spirit Lake Beacon* newspaper ads as "cosy [sic] rooms and homelike fare."[21] On the beach, his guests could rent boats for sailing and rowing, and fishing equipment. The following summer, he opened a pavilion, a spacious two-story building with large windows overlooking the lake. A dining room on the first floor could hold 1,000 chairs in front of a roomy stage. The dining room had a lofty ceiling and a wide staircase that led to 25 "elegantly

---

[21] "Arnolds Park!! (Newspaper advertisement)," *Spirit Lake (Iowa) Beacon*, August 4, 1882: 1

furnished" [22] sleeping rooms on the second floor. His pavilion soon became the center for social events, church and fraternal gatherings, civic speeches and evening dances.

The Chicago, Milwaukee & St. Paul Railway, aware of West Lake Okoboji's appeal and seeing quick profits to be made from trains full of summer tourists, in 1883 extended its line 17 miles north from Spencer, Iowa, to Arnold's park. Visitors no longer had to make the journey over wagon roads that were rugged in fair weather and impassable when wet. They could ride to Arnold's park aboard trains, two every day, every day of the week. Special summer excursions were quickly arranged departing Des Moines, the capital city, at 7 a.m., passing through the population centers of Fort Dodge and Spencer, arriving at Arnold's park at 3 p.m. To accommodate their passengers, the Milwaukee built a hotel next to its depot in Okoboji, and the following summer built and launched a 300-passenger steamer, the *Ben Lennox*. She would be waiting at the dock to provide arriving passengers excursions around the lake.

The first steamer on West Lake Okoboji was the *Favorite*. Built in eastern Iowa where she had worked on the Cedar River, *Favorite* was shipped by rail to Spencer and hauled north to Arnold's park on a pair of horse-drawn wagons. The 30-passenger steamboat was launched in 1881 on West Lake Okoboji. At a time when few roads existed around the lake, the *Favorite* provided transportation to the campgrounds, fishing camps, and early resorts and offered passage north across East Lake Okoboji to the towns of Spirit Lake and Orleans.

A year before the Chicago, Milwaukee & St. Paul reached Arnold's park, the Burlington, Cedar Rapids & Northern Railway arrived in Spirit Lake from the east. The BCR&N, also anticipating the demand for transportation to and accommodations at the Lakes, built a grand hotel, The Orleans, on the shore of Big Spirit Lake. The three-story hotel was 350 feet long and adorned with nine pennant-topped towers. Every one of the 200 guest rooms had a private bath and gas heat, and each had two doors, one leading to the corridor and the other to the 16-foot-wide promenade that overlooked the lake. The railroad launched the *Alpha*, a 45-passenger steamer, to provide its guests with excursions around Big Spirit Lake. Just

---

[22] Untitled editorial, *Spirit Lake Beacon*, June 1, 1883: 3

steps across the isthmus at Orleans, they could board the *Favorite,* or another of a growing fleet of steamboats, and ride to Arnold's park.

To boost passenger traffic, the railroads promoted the Lakes in travel brochures that romanticized the natural charms, accommodations, and recreational opportunities waiting at the Okobojis. BCR&N circulars claimed that for "hunters and anglers there is no place in the Northwest that offers the same inducements as Spirit Lake and East and West Okoboji. Abounding in all variety of fish…even the inexperienced angler will find no difficulty catching."[23] Traveling railroad correspondents Charles B. Holmes & Charles A. Sweetland added in 1885: "West Okoboji is thought by many to be the most beautiful body of water in the United States. Scarcely any one who comes…leaves without carrying a bottle of this fine sand home to show their friends."[24]

Widely read publications such as *Wildwood's Magazine,* which claimed to be the most creditable monthly for gentlemen of wealth and culture, wrote of West Lake Okoboji in 1888 "a host of tourists and sportsmen are attracted to its shores each season by the excellent boating, bathing, shooting, fishing and other recreations of this region. The waters are clear and pure as crystal and in favorable weather, objects may be seen at a great depth below the surface."[25] Methodist Episcopal Bishop John F. Hurst, writing from Okoboji to the *The Iowa State Register—Des Moines,* later known as *The Des Moines Register,* in August 1883, reported, "For real comfort, bracing air, and a rich variety of all the sport that fisherman and hunter could desire, I cannot imagine a more delightful spot than just this."[26]

The promotions were wildly successful, and travelers came by the trainloads. Unable to keep up with the demand for passage aboard the *Alpha,* the BCR&N commissioned a new first-class steamer to serve its Orleans hotel. Her iron parts were shaped and fitted in Dubuque, Iowa. Its woodwork was built at the railroad's car shops in Cedar Rapids, Iowa, and

---

[23] "A Delightful Resort," *Spirit Lake Beacon,* July 21, 1882: 3
[24] Messers Holmes and Sweetland, Special Traveling Press Correspondents of the B.C.R. & N., *"A Descriptive Sketch of the Spirit Lake Region,"* Published in Chicago by The J.M.W. Jones Stationery and Printing Company, 1885: 17
[25] Piscator, Jr., "An Outing in Iowa," *Wildwood's Magazine,* September, 1888: 202
[26] Bishop John F. Hurst, "Life on Okoboji," *The Iowa State Register – Des Moines,* Thursday, August 9, 1883: 4

The Death Boat

then all the sections were shipped to Spirit Lake for assembly. Christened the *Queen,* she was the first steel-hull steamer on the Okobojis. Launched on Big Spirit Lake on July 3, 1883, she could carry 250 passengers.

At Arnold's park, the steamers *Carrie Maxon, Lelia,* and *River Queen* were launched the same year as the *Ben Lennox.* Arriving railroad passengers found an exciting waterfront at Arnold's park. Bathers filled the beach and splashed in the water. Rowboats and sailboats moved across the waters just off shore, and rental boats rested in neat rows on the beach. Visitors saw the fleet of steamers, some boarding at the dock while others waited offshore, black smoke rolling from their stacks and whistles blowing to attract and welcome passengers. After boarding, they could steam across West Lake Okoboji and onto East Lake and north to the towns of Spirit Lake and Orleans. With just a short walk across the isthmus, they might board the *Queen* for a cruise around Big Spirit Lake.

The extremely popular excursions drew thousands to the Lakes, and the hub of all that recreation and transportation was Wesley Arnold's beachfront on West Lake Okoboji, where he was more than happy to provide food, accommodations, and all manner of waterfront recreation.

To celebrate the Fourth of July in 1884, the steamboats offered free rides to arriving railroad passengers at Arnold's park, and Arnold hosted an evening dance in his pavilion. The next summer, he scheduled an all-day Fourth of July celebration that included speeches by local celebrities, sailboat and rowboat races on the water, baseball games in the afternoon, and an evening dance. The next year, the celebration included a spectacular fireworks display launched from the deck of the *Ben Lennox.* As early as 1886, *The Iowa State Register,* was referring to the Lakes area as "this now famous summer resort."[27] The newspaper carried regular reports of activities there and lists of the state's prominent residents traveling to Arnold's park and spending time there.

Adding to the appeal of Arnold's park was the return in 1888 of Abbie Gardner, who opened one of Iowa's first tourist attractions. Now Mrs. Abbie Gardner Sharp, she took up summer residence in her family's cabin,

---

[27] "Information For Everybody Concerning This Famous Summer Resore [*sic*]," *The Iowa State Register – Des Moines,* Tuesday, June 22, 1886: 5

where she sold copies of her book, "History of the Spirit Lake Massacre and the Captivity of Miss Abbie Gardner," as well as postcards and souvenirs. In 1891, she bought the land around the cabin and began lobbying the state legislature for a monument to her family and the settlers killed in the massacre. The legislature appropriated $5,000, and in 1895 the Peterson Granite Company of St. Paul, Minnesota, built the Spirit Lake Massacre Monument adjacent to the Gardner cabin. It was the first legislative-funded monument dedicated in Iowa. With Native American-military clashes still in living memory, Gardner Sharp, her family's cabin, and the popular monument, drew thousands more to the Lakes.

The year after Gardner Sharp moved into the Gardner cabin, Arnold built his famous toboggan slide. The slide was so successful that others were soon built at Crescent Beach, Manhattan Beach and Orleans. In 1898, Arnold topped them all with the tallest chute in the Lakes. He promoted his new attraction with a dazzling Fourth of July fireworks display launched from its peak.

In 1897, when the residents at Arnold's park petitioned the District Court for permission to incorporate, some state newspapers pointed out that the incorporation was simply a way for Arnold's park businesses to capitalize on a loophole in the state's liquor law and sell alcohol in the park. Iowa barred the sale of alcohol except by a licensed pharmacist unless a city allowed it. After the incorporation passed, prohibitionists raised questions about its legality. The General Assembly of Iowa took up the matter and legalized the incorporation May 14, 1897. Arnold, who had been fined $300 in late February for selling liquor illegally, obtained a resolution of consent from the city council, paid the Mulct tax[28], and bought six wagonloads of beer for his Fourth of July celebration.

On Saturday morning, July 3, Oliver Wilson, constable of Center Grove Township, confiscated the beer and hauled the kegs to the Dickinson County Courthouse, where they were locked up in the jail. First thing Monday morning, July 5, the day of the celebration, Arnold got a writ from the clerk of court releasing his beer, and the kegs were returned to the

---

[28] The Mulct Law, passed by the Iowa legislature in 1894, provided, in effect, a local option to allow the sale of alcohol. It didn't repeal Iowa's prohibition against the sale of liquor, but it provided that the law might be violated upon the consent of the community and payment of a certain sum of money, the Mulct Tax. IOWA CODE Sec. 2432 (1897)

amusement park by noon. The celebration that day included morning speakers, music on the lawn by the Spencer, Iowa, military band, dancing to the Ainsworth Orchestra in the pavilion, fireworks, and, as predicted, beer, legally available at 15 cents a glass. An estimated 10,000 people flocked to Arnolds Park for the festivities.

In 1902, Arnold electrified his growing amusement park, mostly to power his winter ice-harvesting business that by 1909 was shipping as many as 400 railroad cars of block ice from the lake each winter. The electric lighting lengthened the days at the park. The warm electric glow of his park could be seen across the lake late into summer evenings. Arnold built a collection of souvenir and refreshment stands on his lakefront, and by the turn of the century the park's reputation as a place for fun and entertainment extended across the Midwest. In 1901, *Billboard Magazine* began listing Arnold's amusement park among the most notable parks, pleasure resorts and summer gardens in the country.[29]

After the turn of the century, Arnold experimented with carnival rides such as the Rolling Wave, a canopied ride similar to a merry-go-round with benches facing to the outside. Alternating sides of the ride rose into the air as it revolved around its center. Loud organ music, perhaps to drown out the machinery that operated it, entertained its riders, and the crowds gathered to watch. Arnold added a bowling alley, roller coaster, roller-skating rink, a carousel he called the Carry-Us-All, a moving-picture show, pool hall, lakeside restaurant and barbershop as he sought to attract and entertain visitors coming by train and steamboat to his lakefront playground.

In 1915, Chicago-based writer and trade newspaper publisher John R. Purchase traveled by train to the Lakes to cover the Iowa State Cleaners and Dyers Association's convention at Spirit Lake. Purchase arrived on Monday, June 21, and attended sessions that afternoon and the following morning. On Tuesday afternoon, he took a break from the meetings to explore the lakes. He boarded the steamboat *Okoboji* at Orleans and later complimented the captain's skillful navigation of the swing bridge at Spirit Lake, The Narrows on East Okoboji, and the second swinging bridge at the entrance to West Lake Okoboji.

---

[29] "Parks," *Billboard (magazine)*, June 8, 1901: 23

The steamer landed at The Inn, Manhattan Beach and the YMCA camp, but as Purchase approached Arnolds Park he was impressed by the large number of cottages on the hills and bluffs behind the park. Drawing closer, he could see a roller coaster rising above the treetops, the carousel on the beach, the crowds gathered at the water's edge, and the toboggan slide shooting bathers into the lake near lines of passengers waiting to board steamers. As the music from the carnival rides and the laughter of bathers playing in the water was carried to him across the water, it was evident to Purchase that he was visiting a different, special kind of place, a place of amusement, celebration, and fun on the order of Coney Island he wrote.[30] His observation, though not the first comparison to Brooklyn, New York's famed oceanfront amusement park, would be used for a decade to describe the special place that Arnolds Park had become.

---

[30] John R. Purchase, "Iowa State Cleaners' and Dyers' Association Fourth Annual Convention," *Cleaning and Dyeing World*, July 15, 1915: 458

The Death Boat

Chapter Three

The Launching of *Miss Thriller*

James Claude Ellis went by J. Claude Ellis, J.C. Ellis and sometimes just Claude Ellis. He was a showman, civic promoter, director of stage shows and public entertainment, and a self-professed entrepreneur. Born in 1875 and raised in Alexandria Bay, he was the son of a carpenter and grew up working in his dad's construction and lumber businesses. In 1907, Ellis started his own business, the first motion-picture theater in Brockville, Ontario, 30 miles west of Alexandria Bay on the Canadian side of the St. Lawrence River. He called it the Theatorium, and he showed three different 20-minute films every week for five cents each.

Motion pictures were new in 1907, and his theater was an instant success. Three years later, he persuaded the village board in Alexandria Bay to allow him to operate a moving-picture theater and a Saturday night amateur vaudeville show in the civic auditorium, Convention Hall. It, too, was a success, and by 1911 Ellis had become manager of Convention Hall. On its stage, he and his wife, Maude, produced live entertainment for local groups, visiting conventioneers and the seasonal tourists who flocked to Alexandria Bay to enjoy the river, its accommodations, and recreation. Ellis occasionally sang on stage, sometimes accompanied by the fire department orchestra.

Ellis also organized, promoted and recruited players for the local baseball and football teams. In 1912, as the leading member of the Alexandria Bay

Board of Trade, he convinced the Van Buren Film Manufacturing Company to film the American Power Boat Association's Gold Cup Races at Alexandria Bay. Ellis used the film, with its aerial and panoramic views of the village, its majestic homes, and beautiful islands and waterways, to promote Alexandria Bay and the Thousand Islands.

The Thousand Islands is a resort destination of almost 2,000 small islands that straddle the U.S.-Canadian border along the St. Lawrence River. At the turn of the century, the area's natural beauty and recreational opportunities drew thousands of tourists and seasonal residents to its grand hotels, world-class inns, privately owned islands, and riverfront castles. The middle-class and wealthy from New York City, Chicago, Cleveland and other cities built summer homes along the shores and on its islands. The area was easily accessible by road, railway, and steamboats. It was a magnet for conventions, business gatherings, and fraternal and lodge associations. The Thousand Islands offered boating, fishing charters, sightseeing tours aboard steamboats and launches, dining on world-class food and luxurious accommodations. Visitors could ferry among the islands to enjoy the spacious porches, sitting rooms, and ballrooms at its riverfront hotels, or play tennis and croquet on their elegant courts.

Alexandria Bay was a picturesque riverfront village at the heart of the Islands. Clustered around the waterfront were seawalls, docks and grand Victorian hotels with names such as Crossmon House, Thousand Island House and Marsden House. They stood four and five stories high and were appointed with sweeping verandas, covered decks, cupolas and pendent-topped spires. The area truly was rich in comfort and recreation.

In 1922, Ellis, a licensed pilot and founding member of the Alexandria Bay Boatmen's Association, began offering high-speed boat rides on a launch he called *Miss Thriller*. She wasn't the first sea sled put into passenger service: rides on a Coney Island sea sled had been available for some time. The preceding summer, a 40-foot sea sled carrying 12 passengers at 42 miles an hour began offering rides from the boardwalk at Atlantic City, New Jersey. But Ellis' purchase was rare and widely reported in the New York newspapers. They reported on his trip to West Mystic to order the boat and its arrival, without engines, the first week of July.

The newspapers reported that Captain Ellis would pilot the new boat himself and that he had obtained the services of Ben Wilbur, known in the Thousand Islands as "the best gas engine man on the river,"[31] to oversee installation of a pair of 300-horsepower Fiat airplane engines. Wilbur was to be the co-pilot of the two-man crew required to operate the sea sled. The newspapers described the boat's every detail, her length and beam, the surface-piercing propellers, the bench seating for the passengers and the pilot and mechanic's positions in the engine compartment. After her debut in August, Ellis offered 20-minute tours of the St. Lawrence from the Cornwall Brothers' dock. He planned to move the boat to Detroit after Labor Day and then on to Miami for the winter. His launch quickly became famous as "the fastest boat in the world carrying passengers for hire."[32] It was widely reported her top speed was 72 miles an hour.

On September 1, 1924, a Monday morning, the hotels—indeed the whole village of Alexandria Bay—was dressed in American flags. Red, white and blue bunting hung from porches, business fronts, public buildings, and street lights in honor of the Labor Day weekend and the following Wednesday's opening of the state American Legion Convention. Bus tours to the village were sold out, and the railroads had added extra sleeping cars for holiday and convention travelers. Hotels and rooming houses throughout the Thousand Islands had been booked for weeks, many with early convention-goers taking advantage of the long weekend. Tourists crowded the four public boat docks on the waterfront all morning. Some shopped or were sightseeing. Others waited to ride the tour boats and talked of golfing, fishing, or canoeing. The play *America*, billed as a thrilling story of love and romance, was scheduled to be onstage at Convention Hall at 2 p.m. In the park, the Lowville (New York) Band was preparing for the evening concert.

Just after 11 a.m., pilot William Certwell turned *Miss Thriller* away from the Cornwall dock and into the St. Lawrence River for its regular tour of the bay. Captain Ellis was seated in the row just ahead of pilot Certwell. Beside him were Charles Jasinski and two members of a German singing society attending a convention at the Thousand Island House. In the row ahead, sat a married couple, Joseph and Flora Weinheimer and their friends

---

[31] "Miss Thriller To Operate At Bay, 70 Miles an Hour Will Be Speed of New Motor Craft." *Thousand Islands Sun (Alexandria Bay, NY)*, Thursday, June 29, 1922: 1
[32] "Fine New Boat On Lake Okoboji," *The Spencer (Iowa) Reporter*, Wednesday, May 6, 1926: 5

Genevieve Fleming and John Mahan, all of Syracuse, New York. Up front were Lillian Lehman, Anne Dabau, Herman Dreiser, and Carl Mantel, all of Brooklyn.

Just as pilot Certwell rounded Sunken Rock Lighthouse and approached Heart Island, one of *Miss Thriller's* driveshafts fractured with a terrifying bang. It threw a large piece of metal through the boat's bottom. Her engines shuddered to a stop and *Miss Thriller* rapidly began filling with water. With no horn or bell aboard and only five life preservers, pilot Certwell commanded, "Everybody get up and yell."[33] At that, some of the passengers began screaming while others called out to shore, a quarter-mile away, for help. Jasinski pulled off his coat, climbed over the passengers in the row ahead of him and onto the bow where he waved the coat toward shore, trying to call attention to the accident. His wife, watching from Cornwall's dock, screamed, pointed to the boat and fainted. Now aware of the accident, pilots in other boats rushed to the scene.

The Thousand Islander, driven by pilot Joe Certwell, William's brother, was first to arrive. When he pulled alongside the boat, *Miss Thriller's* stern was already underwater. He found Jasinski pulling passengers onto the bow of the boat and Ellis, standing in water amidships, pushing passengers forward. At the back of the boat, Joe's brother, in water up to his armpits, was trying to plug the hole with rags and whatever else he could find. With the boat all but lost, pilot William Certwell aimed her toward shallow water, climbed aboard *The Thousand Islander*, and began pulling passengers from the sinking launch. *Miss Thriller* disappeared beneath the water just as her last passenger, Flora Weinheimer, lifted her left foot from the bow. The boat sank in less than five minutes, so fast that passengers scrambling for places on *The Thousand Islander* didn't see her slip away.

Back on shore, some of the passengers were badly frightened, but no one was injured. Ellis left the docks to find someone to recover his boat and efforts began immediately. At first, it appeared *Miss Thriller* settled in the shipping channel, which was more than 100 feet deep, but clever maneuvering by pilot Certwell enabled the launch to catch the edge of Sunken Rock Shoal. The salvage crew found her in only 16 feet of water.

---

[33] "Four Syracusans Face Watery Grave as Boat Sinks in St. Lawrence," *Syracuse (NY) Herald*, Tuesday, September 2, 1924: 4

The crew struggled all day to bring the heavy boat to the surface, and she was finally hauled ashore after dark. Because the repairs to her hull would be complicated, and replacement parts would have to come from the factory, *Miss Thriller* spent the rest of the season in a shed at Captain Joseph Brown's boatyard. Captain Ellis went shopping for a new launch. He would call it *Captain Kidd*.

The Death Boat

Chapter Four

Miss Thriller Moves To Okoboji

John Faust Hafer was born along the banks of the West Branch Susquehanna River, the son of a Pennsylvania Dutch farmer. Some say that even as a boy he dreamed of building boats, but he was raised a farmer, and in 1886 he migrated to central South Dakota. There he tried his hand at homesteading, but after three bad crops, the result of burning winds and ravenous grasshoppers, he walked off the land and moved to Gettysburg, South Dakota. In the community north of the state capital of Pierre and just east of the Missouri River, he found work as a carpenter and learned his way around woodworking tools. He also met and married Charlotte "Lottie" Nordstrom.

John and Lottie soon moved to Pierre where he built a 26-foot boat. Hafer floated his young family down the Missouri River to Yankton, South Dakota, where he hoped to find carpentry work on riverboats. Work was hard to come by, but he heard there was a need for carpenters and opportunities for boat builders at Spirit Lake. Hafer installed a gasoline engine on his boat and sold it for a stake to move his family to the northwest Iowa town. There he hired himself out as a carpenter and began building rowboats in the Warren Paint Shop building.

His boats proved so popular that in three years he built a boathouse in Spirit Lake on the shore of East Lake Okoboji. His rowboats were solid, serviceable and comfortable. They were popular with the locals and visitors who rented them from concessioners along the beaches. At the turn of the century, Hafer began building launches with gasoline engines. His launches were long and extremely narrow to accommodate the heavy engines of the day. His boats had primitive glass jar-encased storage batteries tucked beneath the seats to spark the engines. Boaters had to return to shore before the batteries died and the engine quit.

Hafer boats had V-bottomed hulls and were so heavy they couldn't plane over the water. They were famous for the great wings of spray they threw out to the sides as they plowed through the water with brute force. They were popular from the day his first motor launch appeared on the water. By 1904, almost 100 gasoline launches motored on the Iowa Great Lakes. Six years later *The Spirit Lake Beacon* reported that about 250 motor launches were on the lakes, and many of them were Hafer Craft.

In 1906, Hafer built a launch known for more than a decade as "the fastest launch in the middle west."[34] He named it *White Flyer*. She was 40 feet long, 6 feet wide and powered by an 80-horsepower, four-cylinder Doman engine that weighed almost 2,160 pounds. *White Flyer* reportedly ran 30 miles an hour. In 1909, state Senator Leslie E. Francis of Spirit Lake bought her and renamed her the *Francis Flyer*.

The senator raced her against boats from across the Midwest at events hosted by the Okoboji Yacht Club. Hafer himself often drove the boat in the races. Francis sold his launch in the spring of 1917, and she left the lakes for a new home in northern Minnesota. That same year, the U.S. government, in need of high-quality wooden boats for the war effort, contacted Hafer about building sea sleds for the Navy. Hafer was ready to build the boats, but his shop's capacity and location so far inland prevented an arrangement. At its peak, Hafer's shop built about 15 large motorboats a year.

Charles H. Parker, his wife, Carrie May, and their son, Bill, migrated to Arnolds Park in the late 1890s from Moweaqua, Illinois. An entrepreneur, he rented cottages and rowboats to summer visitors. Parker was among the

---

[34] "Unique Career of John Hafer, The Silent Boatmaker of Okoboji," *The Register and Leader (Des Moines, Iowa),"* Sunday, June 18, 1911: 19

first to put John Hafer's motorboats into passenger launch service. In 1907, he ordered a new Hafer Craft, bought several used Hafers, and built a boat livery for his boats on Lake Minnewashta. From rented dock space at Arnolds Park, he offered motorboat tours around the lake. He called his business The Eagle Line. It was an immediate success.

The season after the *Francis Flyer* left the lakes, Parker contracted Hafer to build an even faster boat. He named the 1918 launch *Red Eagle*, and she was the star of his fleet. With her 125-horsepower engine she was, according to the local newspapers, faster than the *Flyer*. Parker ran The Eagle Line, which included the launches *Ibis, White Eagle, War Eagle, Swan, Dundee, Intruder* and *Tennessee,* for more than 15 years. He became a local hero when he rescued all nine people aboard a burning launch on Okoboji. Owned by another passenger boat operator, Jack Rentz, it had caught fire from an engine backfire. Parker rushed to the scene and transferred Rentz and his eight passengers into the *Ibis*. Several passengers slipped into the water as they scrambled to get off the burning launch, but no one was injured. The fire destroyed the boat.

In June 1921, for reasons that aren't clear, Parker sold his livery and most of his boats. Health issues may have prompted the sale. Both Parker and his wife were in the hospital that spring and the couple was living with their son Bill. Whatever the reason, it seemed to many that Charles Parker was no longer interested in the passenger launch business.

On Saturday morning, July 29, 1922, John W. Hartman purchased a small fleet of launches including most of the former Eagle Line's boats. Hartman had been the mayor of Spirit Lake for more than a decade and owned the city's first automobile dealership. With Parker gone, he saw the opportunity to build a passenger boat business at Arnolds Park around the star of his purchase, *Disturber.*

Disturber, known then as "the fastest boat on the Lakes,"[35] was another Hafer Craft. Built in 1920 for Spencer businessman John J. Hammen, she had a 225-horsepower Sterling engine and Hammen claimed she reached almost 65 miles an hour. With due respect for his boats' heritage, Hartman

---

[35] "J.J. Hammen's New Launch Is The Fastest Boat On The Lakes," *The Spencer (Iowa) News-Herald,* Thursday, August 26, 1920: 4

The Death Boat

called his new company the Eagle Boat Line, and with it he intended to dominate the passenger boating business on West Lake Okoboji. Hartman was an aggressive businessman. He was comfortable giving orders and expected them to be followed. Typically, things went his way. Hartman, who referred to himself as "Old Daddy,"[36] always wore a vested suit sporting a gold chain anchored with a pocket watch. Hartman was not the kind of businessman who could tolerate competition. During the season, he usually could be found along the lakeshore at Arnolds Park overseeing his boats, brass binoculars in hand.

Promoting the Eagle Boat Line began with lakeside construction. Hartman built docks for his boats and connected them with boardwalks. He installed large billboards along his docks showing his rates and advertising his boats, some by name. To further promote his boat line, he worked with local and visiting groups, providing free rides as premiums and prizes for their events. Hartman cleverly advertised his boat line in the local papers by inserting poems under the name Atta Boy. He generated interest and passengers with couplets such as "Their docks and signs are all painted new, take a ride and see what the Eagles can do,"[37]

Hartman was successful. On the Fourth of July, 1923, his boats carried almost 2,000 passengers. On the Fourth of July two years later, the Eagle Boat Line carried more than 3,000 passengers at a dollar a throw. By the end of his first season, Hartman seemed to be well on the way to being the leading passenger boat operator on the lake.

No one still living can explain how two Arnolds Park men, Charles Parker and Lomas Gipner, appeared in Alexandria Bay, New York, in April 1925. What was obvious was that Parker had decided to get back into the passenger launch business and he was there to purchase J. Claude Ellis' sea sled *Miss Thriller*. Gipner was raised on the waters of West Lake Okoboji. Lo, as he was known, was a former hand on the steamer *Okoboji* who had earned his pilot's license while still in his teens. In 1917, Gipner joined the Army and served as a pilot with the 17th Aero Squadron in France. After the war, he returned to the Lakes and signed on with the Milford Aero Club,

---

[36] "Court Hears Testimony in Okoboji Case," *The Daily Iowan (Iowa City)*, Wednesday, December 11, 1929: 1
[37] "The Eagle Boat Line," *The Milford Mail*, Thursday, May 28, 1925: 7

flying sightseeing excursions over West Lake Okoboji. It must have seemed obvious to Parker that Gipner was the ideal co-pilot for the two-handed sea sled *Miss Thriller*.

By month's end, Parker and Gipner had completed the purchase of *Miss Thriller*, including the rights to retain use of the name. They arranged transportation for the boat from Alexandria Bay to Clayton, New York, where she was loaded onto a railroad car and sent on an eight-day journey to Arnolds Park. Before she left Clayton, the *Watertown Standard* reported that *Miss Thriller*, "a favorite attraction at Alexandria Bay,"[38] was moving to West Lake Okoboji, Iowa.

Miss Thriller arrived Tuesday, May 5, 1925. Resting on the railcar, the strange-looking launch must have been quite an attraction. It was far different from the long, narrow Hafer Craft that were so common in the lakes area. During the war, the state's daily newspapers reported the Navy's use of sea sleds. After the war, magazines such as *MotorBoating*, *Popular Mechanics* and *Scientific American* published stories about their peacetime developments as fast, safe and dry "motorcars-of-the-sea."[39] When the Coast Guard began buying the high-speed boats to challenge rum-runners, sea sleds were back in the newspapers again.

Here, sitting at the Arnolds Park depot, was the first sea sled anyone in northwest Iowa, and perhaps the entire Midwest, had ever seen. With its funny-looking hull, twin engines, large propellers that clearly didn't reach completely into the water, and a pair of bug-eyed headlights, it would have been easy to believe she was formerly a military craft. In fact, most people already believed what newspapers later incorrectly reported about the launch, that she was a "government-built submarine chaser" refitted for passenger use.[40]

The Spencer Reporter broke the story of *Miss Thriller's* arrival. The article on the bottom of Page 9 reported the basics: her Alexandra Bay heritage, her

---

[38] "*Miss Thriller*, Widely Known Along River, Carries Thrill Seekers to Death," *Watertown (NY) Standard*, Tuesday, July 30, 1929: 1
[39] "MOTOR CAR OF THE SEA," *The Naples (NY) News*, Wednesday, December 29, 1915: 6
[40] "PROBE OF OKOBOJI TRAGEDY BEGINS," *The Des Moines (Iowa) Register*, Tuesday, July 30, 1929: 1

width and length, and a description of her twin engines. But what most interested the readers was her reported speed, 75 miles an hour. That was faster than land travel over Iowa roads or rails. The next day, *The Spirit Lake Beacon* put the story on its front page and announced that Parker planned to launch *Miss Thriller* on West Lake Okoboji the upcoming weekend.

A large crowd gathered Sunday, May 10, on the docks and along the shore to see *Miss Thriller* take her first loops around the lake. They watched as her signature rooster tail shot high into the air and then she lurched forward and raced across the water faster than any other boat ever seen on the Lakes. The display left no doubt *Miss Thriller* was going to be one sensational attraction. The headline in *The Milford Mail* following her debut read simply "Fastest Boat On Earth," and the story went on to declare her the "fastest commercial passenger boat in the world."[41]

Miss Thriller races across West Lake Okoboji.
Courtesy of the Iowa Great Lakes Maritime Museum

Parker leased space on the beach at Arnolds Park and, taking advantage of all the free publicity, put up a sign on the end of his dock that read *"Miss Thriller, That Fast Boat."*[42] Business was brisk. Her novel shape, speed, and just plain curiosity made *Miss Thriller* an immediate star. On her first Fourth of July in Iowa, long lines of passengers waited for a ride. But her success came at a cost: John Hartman's Eagle Boat Line began losing business to the new launch.

When Hartman bought Parker's boats, Arnolds Park had only a handful of launch operators. Most owned one boat, perhaps two. Hartman hoped his

---

[41] "Fastest Boat On Earth," *The Milford Mail,* Thursday, May 14, 1925: 1
[42] Unknown photographer, *"The Eagle Boat Line Docks, 1928,"* Dickinson County Museum, Spirit Lake, Iowa, Deater, (1979), former catalogue no. 624

well-run Eagle Boat Line would put them out of business. Now, with Parker back on the lake with an immensely popular launch, his plans were threatened. Tempers flared and such a heated animosity developed between the frustrated Hartman and confident Parker that in mid-July boat Inspector Jacob "Jake" B. Thompson wrote Governor John Hammill, "There is such a rivalry between Hartman and Parker that, by their operation of their fast boats on West Okoboji, lives might be endangered."[43] Hammill encouraged Thompson to confront the men with his concerns, and while he might have, the rivalry persisted as the two owners challenged one another for every passenger all season long.

The following winter, Hartman went shopping for a launch to compete with *Miss Thriller*. He found what he wanted in Minneapolis in a boat he called *Teaser*, a handsome launch of solid mahogany and leather upholstery. Thirty-three feet long, she could carry 25 passengers, and, more important to Hartman, had a 12-cylinder 500-horsepower engine. He claimed she would run 60 miles an hour. *Teaser* went into the water in May 1926.

To promote his boat, Hartman added new signage to his docks that not only prominently displayed her name and her mile-a-minute claim but also conveniently obscured *Miss Thriller's* dock down the beach. Other signs boasted that his boats were "faster than any [other] boats on the lake for the same money."[44] And he staged a dramatic stunt to promote his new launch. Never identified by any other name, Dare Devil Dan leaped from a low-flying airplane onto the deck of *Teaser* as they raced, one in the air and one on the water, across West Lake Okoboji. The leap was a spectacular and crowd-thrilling promotion for John Hartman's Eagle Boat Line.

While competition raged between John Hartman on one end of the beach and Charles Parker on the other, the state of Iowa waded into a more urgent problem, one that would change the look of the waterfront at Arnolds Park and put the rival owners' docks adjacent to one another on the beach.

After Wesley Arnold's death in 1905, his amusement park was divided in half and passed to his daughters. Hattie and her husband, Dr. Alonzo L.

---

[43] State Boat Inspector J.B. Thompson to Governor John Hammill, July 16, 1925 TS
[44] Unknown photographer, *"The Eagle Boat Line Docks, 1928,"* Dickinson County Museum, Spirit Lake, Iowa, Deater, (1979), former catalogue no. 624

Peck, inherited the park on the north side of Lake Street. Luella and Mabel got the property on the south side of the street. Luella's husband, Arthur O. Stevens, operated it for more than a decade and then sold it to Carsten P. Benit in 1918. Through the years, Stevens, Benit and Peck built a collection of souvenir and refreshment stands, a lakefront store, and boathouses and bathhouses along the beach and out over the water on stilts.

Just before the Fourth of July in 1926, Peck roped off the public beach to keep the nonpaying public away. The beach was state property, the state had sovereignty over the lake and shore up to the high-water mark. That meant Peck couldn't legally bar the public from the beach. Complaints reached the state conservation board almost overnight. The board contacted the Iowa attorney general, and he sent Assistant Attorney General Neill Garrett to the lake to protect the state's interest.

Garrett arrived Friday morning, July 2, to find the beach roped off. He reported his findings to the board and, at its urging, searched for a judge who might order Peck to open the beach to the public. The three judges in the 14th Judicial District were Daniel D. Coyle, Fred C. Davidson and James DeLand. Judge DeLand was in session at Storm Lake, 55 miles away. Garrett drove to Storm Lake and at 5 p.m. that afternoon the judge issued an order enjoining Peck from denying the public free access to the beach. Garrett and the board had saved the holiday for the public. *The Spencer News-Herald* reported more than 50,000 people spent the weekend at the Lakes, where they had free access to the beach at Arnolds Park.

The order was never made permanent; instead, at the conservation board's request, the Iowa Legislature passed an act that gave the board the duty to adopt and enforce any rules and regulations necessary to protect the public's access to the state's waters. The act went further, prohibiting the building or construction of any structures on or over state-owned beaches or waters. It gave the board the power to order the removal of buildings already in place. The 42nd General Assembly deemed the matter so important that the act was to go into effect as soon it could be published in the local newspaper, *The Spirit Lake Beacon*.

The act was printed April 7, 1927. Twenty-nine days later, the conservation board gave Peck, Benit, Parker, Hartman and all others 30 days to remove their structures from the lakefront. Peck and Benit were allowed to keep one bathhouse and one seasonal dock each. As a result, the steamboats moved to the dock on Benit's lakefront. The speedboat operators, who had to obtain seasonal permits from the state boating inspector and leases from Peck, moved to docks they built on Peck's lakefront. The Eagle Boat Line docks and *Miss Thriller's* dock, which Parker shared with launch operator Roy Lombard, were now adjacent to one another on the waterfront.

With Hartman and Parker now in one another's face, the quarreling escalated and spread out onto the water when Hartman ordered his pilots to run alongside *Miss Thriller,* interrupting the sea sled's operation with rocking waves and heavy splashing. The rivalry for customers was so keen that soon pilots on both sides, according to Harry Wilsey, an Eagle Boat Line pilot who later served as a deputy sheriff in nearby Clay County, were taking unnecessary risks with the speedboats.

Inspector Thompson became concerned the rivalry was putting the passengers' safety at risk. He wrote to the governor July 27, 1927, the morning after a confrontation at the docks had come to fisticuffs, that the owners of the boat lines "have conducted themselves as to bring considerable discredit upon themselves and the resort." Their behavior, he continued, "is not only foolhardy, but it jeapordizes [*sic*] the lives of the passengers."[45] With Thompson unable or unwilling to stop the fighting, it festered the rest of the season.

In March of 1927, Parker and his son Bill traveled to Rio Linda, California, and bought four tracts of land where they planned to plant orchards. They were going to become fruit growers. On their return to the Lakes, Parker began selling off his Arnolds Park properties. At the end of the 1927 season, he sold his rental cottages and *Miss Thriller* and moved his family to California. *Miss Thriller's* new owner, Frank Leslie Clark, known to his friends as Let Clark, was a farmer, businessman and occasionally an exhibition boxer. He stepped deep into the middle of the struggle with Hartman, who was as determined as ever to eliminate the smaller operators and may have thought Clark was a lesser opponent than Parker.

The summer of 1928 provided a very public window into the spat between the two boat owners. The first glimpse was in July. As part of its annual

---

[45] State Boat Inspector J.B. Thompson to Governor John Hammill, July 27, 1927 TS

picnic, *The Sioux City Tribune* invited the country's fastest motorboats to compete in its speedboat races at Triboji Beach. Clark promised to be there and he challenged all comers to a head-to-head race. His challenge, of course, was directed at Hartman and his *Teaser*. Clark and *Miss Thriller* spent the day at Triboji, where they gave rides to picnic-goers and waited for a response that never came. All Clark could do was have his pilot, Pete Eckman, demonstrate *Miss Thriller's* speed and performance in a crowd-thrilling display.

A week after the *Tribune's* picnic, Hartman issued a challenge of his own. He had installed a 350-horsepower engine in *Red Devil*, probably Parker's renamed *Red Eagle*, and he claimed it was the fastest boat on the lake—aside from *Teaser*, of course. Hartman backed up his challenge with cash. According to *Roof Garden News*, the amusement park's newspaper, he put up $1,000 in cash to match any purse in a head-to-head race. Clark never responded to Hartman's challenge for the same reason that Hartman had ignored Clark the week earlier: Neither owner wanted to prove the other man right.

While the public saw harmless challenges and showmanship, a much darker battle heated up between the boat owners. *Miss Thriller's* continuing success frustrated Hartman so much that he once chased the launch all over the lake in one of his own boats. He threw broad waves across her bow, rocking *Miss Thriller* and knocking her passengers about. Later, he ordered his pilots to zigzag in front of the sea sled to prevent her from passing as she made her tours. Hartman eventually ordered pilot Roy Lombard, who now worked for Hartman, to swamp *Miss Thriller* by throwing his wake into the launch while she was at her dock. Lombard protested but did as he was ordered. The wake filled *Miss Thriller* and she sank, tied to the dock. Hartman's son Milo, who worked as a pilot for the Eagle Boat Line, snapped a picture of the boat lying on the bottom of the lake.

Late in the 1928 boating season, Inspector Thompson put a stop to the rivalry. He did so not by confronting the boatmen but by revoking *Miss Thriller's* license. On one of her tours, *Miss Thriller* leaked water deep enough to stall her engines. Water had to be pumped out of the launch before she could be towed back to shore. An inspection by Thompson revealed rotting framing in her hull. The source of the water is unclear, perhaps a failure of the repair at Alexandria Bay or maybe poor maintenance since, but the boating inspector ordered her off the water. Hartman suddenly found himself with exactly what he wanted, almost all the passenger launch business at Arnolds Park. In the spring of 1929, he reached for the rest. He negotiated leases with Peck and Benit for exclusive rights to the waterfront at Arnolds Park. It was an idea that had been tried before.

The Death Boat

Chapter Five

Boat Line Warfare

In May 1886, brothers Alphonso and Elmer Henderson built a new, larger dock on Wesley Arnold's waterfront to replace the one where the *Favorite* had been boarding passengers since 1881. The former dock was no longer large enough for the growing numbers of steamboats that were using the dock. For almost a decade, the boatmen shared the expenses of maintaining the Henderson-built dock on Arnold's property while sharing the lucrative passenger business.

In April 1895, that all changed. Captain Herman Mills and Captain John Allen, owners of the steamers *Hiawatha* and *Milwaukee*, leased exclusive rights to the lakeshore from Arnold. Mills and Allen tore down the Hendersons' dock and erected a dock that they refused to allow other boatmen to use. They turned down offers to pay for extending the dock to accommodate more steamboats, just as they turned down offers to pay for landing privileges. When boatmen tried to use the dock anyway, Mills and Allen obtained an injunction in District Court, blocking the boarding or unloading passengers from their dock.

The barred owners were forced to move their boats farther north along the shore to what was known as the Manhattan Pier, too far away to appeal to visitors. The move threatened to put them out of business. William Evans and George McCutchin, owners of the *Huntress*, and the Henderson brothers, who had launched the new steamer *Iowa* that season, appealed the injunction to the Iowa Supreme Court. They maintained the dock built in

1886 had become public property because of its long-term use without objection from Arnold. They contended that its replacement should be too. Mills and Allen argued that Arnold owned the property and had the right to engage in an exclusive lease if he chose. The Supreme Court agreed with the lower court's decision. Evans, McCutchin, the Hendersons and the other steamboat operators were forced to leave Arnolds Park. The sting lingered among the boatmen for years. Arguing their case was a 25-year-old attorney only three years out of law school, Leslie E. Francis, a future state senator from Dickinson County.

Fifteen years later, boatmen were in court fighting over lake access again. An extended drought in the 1890s lowered the water in the lakes dramatically, and the once popular and lucrative cruises between Arnolds Park, Spirit Lake and Orleans came to an end. As early as 1894, the *Ben Lennox,* by then renamed the *Manhattan,* could no longer navigate East Lake. By the turn of the century, none of the steamers were able to make the passage. Without the popular excursions to Arnolds Park, guests at the Hotel Orleans dropped off dramatically. In 1898, the Burlington, Cedar Rapids & Northern Railway closed the hotel. The next year, the railroad tore it down and sold the *Queen.*

In winter 1900, the *Queen's* new owners, planning to operate her on West Lake Okoboji, hauled the steamer over the isthmus onto East Lake Okoboji. There, she broke through the ice and settled to the bottom of the shallow lake. She lay flooded and frozen into the ice until the new owners sold her to the Hendersons. The Hendersons chopped her out of the ice, pumped out the water, and hauled her to their boatyard in Okoboji. She was refitted and put into service the following summer.

Two years later, the Okoboji Steamboat Company was incorporated, and Captain Fred Roff, pilot of the *Okoboji,* was enlisted to manage the company. The company acquired the *Okoboji, Queen, Iowa, Illinois* and *Hiawatha* and negotiated landing rights at Arnolds Park and points across West Lake Okoboji. In 1903, with high water returning, the *Queen,* piloted by Charles Gipner, Lo's older brother, became the first steamer to again reach Spirit Lake. The steamboat company quickly added docks at Spirit Lake and Orleans.

In summer 1910, Charles Parker began picking up and dropping off passengers on the Okoboji Steamboat Company docks around the lakes. Unable to keep Parker off its docks, the steamboat company went to court seeking an injunction prohibiting Parker from using its docks to conduct his business. The court granted the injunction. If Parker wanted to ferry passengers directly to the landings, shortcutting the long steamboat routes, he would have to lease his own accesses. Parker apparently abandoned the idea, and for the next 20 years, boatmen accommodated one another as they competed for passengers on the lakefront at Arnolds Park.

In spring 1929, *Miss Thriller* was in the care of two new pilots, Frank Long and Jasper "Jap" Alexander. Long grew up in Pipestone, Minnesota. He was a former race car driver, launch operator, automobile mechanic, and engine inspector for the Rock Island Railroad. Alexander was an Arnolds Park native who served with Lo Gipner in France. Before the war, he was a mechanic, and on his return he went to work at the amusement parks where he managed various concessions and the roller-skating rink. Long and Alexander had an arrangement with Richard "Dick" Davis of Milford, Iowa, to pay for the boat in installments while they operated her on the lake. Davis, an agent for the Milford bank, had acquired *Miss Thriller* through foreclosure.

Working at Wilson Boat Works, they repaired the launch, remounted the engines and installed a larger pair of battery-operated headlights. Thompson inspected their work while it was underway and licensed the boat July 1. Long's pilot license had expired, so Thompson issued him a new one at the same time. The sea sled was launched the next day.

That summer, with his exclusive leases in hand, Hartman expanded his operation on the waterfront at Arnolds Park. He had four docks, three in front of Peck's property, each about 40 feet apart, the fourth in front of Benit's amusement park. The docks were five planks wide and long enough to park four launches, two on each side. A two-plank walkway ran the length of the shoreline connecting the docks. Some sections of the boardwalk had handrails. Near the walk's south end was a building Hartman used for an office; near the north end was a shelter with benches. The shelter's roof rested on tall dock posts. At a booth in the center of the boardwalk, tickets could be bought for any of Hartman's boats for $1 each. His launches that season included *Teaser* and five Hafer Craft: *Blue Streak,*

The Death Boat

Red Devil, Zipper, Cannon Ball and *Spitfire.*

At 5:30 a.m. July 1, 1929, Frank Long, Jap Alexander, Roy Lombard, who now owned the launches *Red Mahogany* and *Sea Gull*, and Lo Gipner, who was piloting for Lombard, pulled down one of Hartman's large advertising signs. They sawed through his handrails and constructed a dock from Lake Street, over the top of Hartman's boardwalk, and out into the lake. Newspapers later described what followed as outright "Boat Line Warfare."[46] News stories, open letters, witness testimony, and court transcripts recorded the details.

The waterfront at Arnolds Park during the summer of 1928. John Hartman, center, leans on the Eagle Boat Line ticket booth. *Zipper* is the third launch right of Hartman, somewhat obscured by a utility pole. *Miss Thriller's* dock, with its overhead sign, is left behind Hartman's lakeshore office. In the background is the steamboat *Queen*.
Courtesy of The Dickinson County Museum

At sunrise, Hartman saw what had happened to his property. He was enraged. He demanded the men remove the dock and repair the damage. No one, he told them, had the right to build through his property. His leases with Peck and Benit barred any other passenger launch operators on the waterfront. Long, Alexander, and Lombard ignored the damage to Hartman's operation and claimed their dock was not on Peck or Benit property but on city property, the extension of Lake Street, and they had permission from City Council members and the state board of conservation to build a dock there.

Hartman summoned Mayor Bart J. Lawler and had him order the

---

[46] "9 Dead In Okoboji Boat Crash," *The Graettinger (Iowa) Times,* Thursday, August 1, 1929: 1

"independent boatmen"[47] to remove the dock. They told the mayor his orders were "not worth a God damn" and he could "go to Hell."[48] Hartman threatened to have the dock ripped out if they didn't remove it; indeed, three years earlier, another dock built from Lake Street had been torn out. Long and Lombard put the dock under 24-hour watch and began taking turns spending nights there.

In the face of daily threats to drive them out of business, Long and Alexander began selling tickets and boarding passengers across Hartman's boardwalk. Hartman and his son Milo responded by calling the men "God damn sons of bitches," "dirty cowards," and "sneaky crooks."[49] John Hartman intimidated their passengers with insulting remarks, some of which witnesses later would hesitate to repeat in court. This time, Long went to the mayor for help and asked Lawler to put a stop to the abuse of his passengers. The mayor refused, saying "the public gets a kick" out of the scene the Hartmans were creating.[50]

Hartman lowered the price of his tickets to 75 cents to undercut the independents. Long and Alexander reduced the cost of their tickets to match the price. On Sunday, July 14, Hartman created such a scene that Long called the sheriff. Hartman was arrested and charged with using abusive language directed at Long and Alexander and public intoxication. Hartman pleaded guilty to intoxication and paid the fine and costs.

By now, the amusement park owners Peck and Benit had waded into the fight. They protested the use of a public street to do business. *Miss Thriller's* dock, they said, had been built to take advantage of the crowds their parks brought to the waterfront and Long and Alexander shouldn't be able to operate there for free. The Arnolds Park water tank was on Peck's property and newspaper reports said he threatened to cut off the city's water supply unless officials had the dock removed. Peck denied saying any such thing, but he insisted that any dock, even on Lake Street, would need a permit

---

[47] "Sidelights Regarding the Lakes Tragedy," *The Spencer News-Herald,* Thursday, August 1, 1929: 1
[48] Statement of Facts, Appellant's Brief and Argument from Dickinson County District Court, Iowa v. Milo Hartman (Aug. 26, 1931): 5
[49] Testimony of Mrs. Nan Meade: Arguments on Point Three, Appeal from Dickinson County District Court, Iowa v. Milo Hartman (August, 1931): 20
[50] "Who Was To Blame," *Spirit Lake Beacon,* Thursday, January 23, 1930: 4

from the conservation board, and he knew none had been issued. Board Chairman W.E.G. Saunders had given Long and Alexander permission to build and use their dock until the board reviewed their request, but the board had yet to discuss the matter.

With that, Long and Alexander hired Spirit Lake lawyer Kenneth B. Welty. On Monday morning, July 15, they went to the state board of conservation's regular meeting in Algona, Iowa. Peck and his attorney, Harry E. Narey, followed them to urge the board to deny a permit.

The board was attending the dedication of a new state park that day and referred the matter to a committee. Board members were chosen and directed to inspect the dock the following Sunday and report back to the board. First, the inspection was delayed, and then the report was put off until Friday, July 26.

In the meantime, the confrontation on the waterfront escalated. In front of large crowds along the beach, Milo Hartman had taken to using a megaphone to hurl insults at Long and Alexander. He claimed the Eagle Boat Line would run them out of business, go after Lombard next, and would soon own the steamboat company too. Milo Hartman began confronting *Miss Thriller* ticket buyers, telling them that Long and Alexander ran a "tramp boat line."[51] *Miss Thriller,* he warned, was "just a pile of junk; she had sunk in the Saint Lawrence River and her bottom was covered with patches."[52] He showed them his picture of *Miss Thriller* swamped at her dock as proof she was not safe to ride, and he shouted at passengers boarding *Miss Thriller* that "nobody but bootleggers and prostitutes ride that boat."[53]

The confrontations were so harassing that passengers aboard *Miss Thriller* were seen climbing from their seats and walking off the dock, abandoning their ride. And the price-cutting continued. By the last week of July, passengers were paying just 25 cents to ride the launches.

---

[51] State v. Hartman, 233 N.W. 533 (Dec. 1930): 2
[52] United States Law Review, Vol. 65: 205
[53] Vernon Titterington, Dickinson District Court Transcript of Evidence Before the Grand Jury, State of Iowa vs. John and Milo Hartman, Case File 40360, RG 55 Iowa Supreme Court, State Historical Society of Iowa.

On Friday, July 26, the state conservation board put off the discussion of a permit for *Miss Thriller's* dock until the following Monday. On Saturday, July 27, at Peck's request, the District Court in Spirit Lake issued an injunction, restraining Long and Alexander from soliciting passengers for their speedboat on the beach in front of his property. Within hours, however, neither decision would matter to *Miss Thriller*.

The Death Boat

Chapter Six

The Day of the Accident

By 1929, West Lake Okoboji was a seasoned resort destination hosting thousands of summer residents, vacationers and weekend visitors. It was a popular gathering place for family reunions, business conventions, church retreats, and sporting clubs. Summer homes had replaced many of the seasonal cottages, and large resorts offered the finest accommodations.

Terrace Park Beach was home to The Casino Ballroom, a spacious two-story building with tall white pillars supporting long, wide porches on the second floor. The first floor offered dressing rooms, a dining room, and a popular soda fountain. The second floor had a large ballroom. Grand doorways that opened onto awning-shaded porches, overlooking the lawn, lined the ballroom's south wall. Across the dance floor, more than two dozen tall, narrow windows overlooked the lake. The casino had its own newspaper, *Casino Courier*, which profiled its orchestras, highlighted upcoming groups, and promoted its concession stand and waterslide on the beach.

To the north, on the west side of the lake, the Manhattan Beach Hotel was built across the beach. Each room had its own view of the water. Hattie P. Elston wrote that people considered the hotel rather showy with its long porch lined with rocking chairs.[54] The Manhattan's dining and ballroom, where evening clothes were the rule at dinner, stretched out over the lake on stilts. The hotel had a bowling alley and, on the beach, a bathhouse and toboggan slide.

On Dixon Beach, northwest across the lake from Arnolds Park, stood The Inn. Its first quarters were host to guests before the turn of the century. It had grown through the years into an elegant complex of buildings with spacious decks and verandas. A canopy of mature oak trees shaded a grand wooden stairway leading down to the beach. Its Tea Room was almost as famous as the Inn's pavilion, a two-story ballroom that, like the Manhattan's, was built over the water on the lakefront.

Highways and hard-surfaced roads now reached all the resorts, eating establishments, and recreational centers. The remaining steamboats—*Queen, Des Moines,* and *Sioux City*—offered sightseeing tours from Arnolds Park and passage to the resorts, conveniently scheduled to accommodate the evening ballroom dances.

The amusement parks had matured as well. They were the home of the Pippin Coaster, The Majestic and the Roof Garden, the largest roller coaster, largest roller-skating rink and the largest dance floor in Iowa. They were also the home of the Park Theatre and the Fun House with its trick mirrors, shifting floors and barrel roll. New that summer in Peck's Amusement Park was the Midway Circle with a shooting gallery, miniature railway depot and automatic baseball machines.

Together, Peck's Amusement Park and the Benit Amusement Park boasted the latest in carnival rides, including a Ferris wheel and bumper cars, a penny arcade, and games of skill and chance. There were concession and souvenir stands, soda fountains, candy shops, a drug store, and a restaurant. On Sunday evenings, when the parks hosted their largest crowds, the smells of sweet and greasy foods filled the air. So did the sounds of carnival machinery, amplified music, and midway barkers.

Sunday, July 28, 1929, promised to be another high-energy day at the lake. The sky was clear, as it had been all week. Iowans were enduring a

---

[54] Elston, Hattie P., *White Men Follow After: A Collection of Stories About the Okoboji-Spirit Lake Region*. Athens Press, Iowa City, Iowa, 1946: 70

record-breaking heat wave, but the temperature was forecast to be 92 degrees, the lowest daytime temperature in a week. The winds had subsided Saturday evening and were expected to remain calm till Monday. Conditions were perfect for the large crowds expected on the last Sunday in July.

At its annual picnic, *The Sioux City Tribune* planned a full schedule of events. Starting at noon, there would be a parade, beauty pageant, swimming competition and motorboat races. The Le Mars (Iowa) Municipal Band was providing the music for the day and state aviatrix Muriel Hanford would be looping over the crowd in her two-passenger Stearman biplane on her way to the picnic. Riding in the seat in front of her was Miss Sioux City, Fern Layer, mistress of ceremonies for the pageant.

Across the lake, Stanley's Aristocrats were playing at The Casino. Harold Austin and his New Yorkers were on stage at the Central Pavilion on the lakeshore north of Arnolds Park. Opening at the Park Theatre that night was the silent movie "The Pagan," starring "The Latin Lover" Ramon Novarro. Cato's Vagabonds, a 10-piece orchestra from Des Moines and one of the most popular bands in the Midwest, was playing at The Roof Garden.

Among the thousands who planned to spend the day at the lake were James and Naomi Adams of Keota, Iowa. They got up early Sunday to make the 300-mile drive to Arnolds Park. They were going to meet Flave and Alcy Hagist and Dorothy Clark, who had driven up Saturday. The women were Naomi's sisters. James and Naomi had to work Saturday, the biggest day of the week for their dry-cleaning business. They stayed until closing and made the seven-hour trip first thing in the morning with their 5-year-old son, Tommy.

Lloyd and Mary Cummings left about 6:30 Sunday morning for Arnolds Park from Wabasso, a small town near Redwood Falls in southwestern Minnesota. They were accompanied by Mary's sister Ethel Heathcock and friends Mary Thompson and Clarence Nesburg. They planned to celebrate Lloyd's birthday. He had turned 32 on Friday.

Philip and Jessie Schneider and a party of friends had driven to the

The Death Boat

Lakes on Saturday from Hinton, Iowa, just outside of Sioux City. They were making a weekend of their visit.

Just before noon Sunday, Melvin Keohnk and his sweetheart, Luella Adams, headed northeast for a 25-mile drive from their homes in Everly, Iowa, to the Lakes. They told friends they were going to spend part of the afternoon swimming at Terrace Park Beach, and then they were going to the amusement parks to ride the speedboat *Thriller*. When they arrived at Arnolds Park, hundreds of people filled the amusement parks. Others were picnicking by their cars or under the trees along the shore, and some were rowing rented boats offshore. The water was filled with bathers. Keohnk and Adams felt lucky to find an open parking place that time of day. It was on Lake Street between the Benit and Peck parks, smack in the middle of the fun.

Speedboat vendors were doing brisk business on the lakefront. Even with the swirl of the rivalry, *Miss Thriller* was having her best day ever. Just before 9 p.m., about 40 minutes after sunset, the parks were alive with the sounds of festive music, roaring crowds, and the clatter and whir of carnival rides. The blinking lights of the rides and flashing lamps of the arcades lit the parks with a glow that began to overtake the fading traces of daylight as four friends from Linn Grove, Iowa, about 40 miles south of the Lakes, stepped onto the docks along the beach. They were planning to end their evening with a speedboat ride. Milo Nelson and Thomas Christian had driven to Arnolds Park earlier in the day, where they met their friends Esther Rehnstrom and Helga Hansen. The girls were spending the summer at the Lakes. Rehnstrom recently had taken a job at Arnolds Park and was living with the H.C. Walters family. Hansen was working for and living with the Ralph Clinton family. They had been dancing at the Roof Garden and now were going to ride *Miss Thriller*.

As they passed the Eagle Boat Line boats, Milo Hartman approached Helga Hansen and told her that he wouldn't ride in *Miss Thriller*. She had sunk once on the St. Lawrence River and twice in West Lake Okoboji, he said. He didn't think the boat was safe to ride. The four friends talked it over and decided to ride *Miss Thriller* anyway. They bought tickets from Pete Eckman and took all four seats in the second row because a couple, Koehnk and Adams, occupied two of the four seats in the front row. Lloyd and Mary Cummings, eventually joined Koehnk and Adams up front.

Eckman sold a pair of tickets to an acquaintance, Henry Hintz, and Hintz's friend Lucille Patterson, and he introduced them to pilot Frank Long, who was preparing for the ride. They sat in the third row on the left side.

John and Gustie Steinke and their son, Arnold, from the tiny Iowa town of May City, a short distance west of the Lakes, walked down to the beach to ride *Miss Thriller* that Sunday evening at Eckman's invitation. Both men were auctioneers, and Eckman had offered the Steinkes a ride in the boat. John, Gustie, and Arnold had spent the afternoon at the parks and had been talking about the ride all day. Gustie refused to go out on the water, but John and Arnold planned to ride. As they walked out on the dock and looked at the sea sled, John changed his mind; he wasn't going to ride the boat either. He and Gustie would watch from shore and wait for Arnold to return. Arnold took the seat in the third row next to Hintz, who had traded places with his friend, Lucille, so she could ride on the outside.

Guy Hedrick, a friend of Long's, sat in the back row on the left. Friends Kenneth Darlington, 11, and Roy Barnes, 9, had gone to the waterfront planning to ride another boat. Barnes already had a ticket for *Blue Streak*, but they decided to pool their money and buy tickets for *Miss Thriller*. They sat one behind the other, Kenneth in the third row next to Arnold Steinke and Roy in the back row next to Hedrick.

Just as Long pulled *Miss Thriller* away from the dock, Neal Gelino, the 11-year-old son of a park concessionaire and a friend of *Miss Thriller's* co-pilot Jap Alexander, jumped aboard. He frequently rode in empty seats for free, and on this ride sat next to his friend Roy. *Miss Thriller*, who could carry 16 passengers and two crewmen, left Arnolds Park with 17 on board. As she departed, John and Gustie Steinke watched and waved at Arnold. It was the last time they would see their son alive.

Miss Thriller's tour was a 20-minute counter-clockwise loop through the middle of West Lake Okoboji. Pilot Long left the dock going northwest through Cass Bay and past Fort Dodge Point to his right. He eased the boat to the right, north, and toward the lights of The Inn on Dixon Beach. Nearing The Inn, he turned left, running west along Dixon Beach, past Atwell Point, and across the middle of the lake toward the Manhattan Beach Hotel on the west shore. Approaching the hotel, he made his last turn, a long left turn of more than 130 degrees that pointed *Miss Thriller* back to the lights of Arnolds Park. He was returning to shore.

As Long finished his last turn, James and Naomi Adams, who were seated in the back seat of the Eagle Boat Line launch *Zipper*, caught sight of *Miss Thriller's* distinctive twin headlights as their pilot, Harold Yarns, backing *Zipper* from her mooring facing the beach, turned toward the middle of the lake. The Adamses had wanted to ride *Miss Thriller,* but she had already left the dock when Naomi's sister Dorothy Clark agreed to take Tommy to the merry-go-round so they could ride a motorboat. Neither of the Adamses had ever seen a lake as big as West Okoboji and they were apprehensive about the ride as they climbed aboard. James helped Naomi put on her life preserver. A strap broke as James pulled his on, so Yarns handed him another.

Pilot Yarns, who was 23, had grown up wrangling boats for his father, Bert Yarns, owner of Angler's Bay Resort on Big Spirit Lake, but Sunday was his first day alone as a licensed pilot. This would be his second trip since sunset. It was dark as he left the dock; only the lingering light in the sky and its reflection on the water enabled him to discern the horizon across the lake.

Seated in the row ahead of James and Naomi Adams was the Schneider party: Jessie Schneider; son Philip, 4; granddaughter Patricia, 5; and her niece Jean Ellison, 16. Ellison was taking her second motorboat ride of the day; she had ridden *Miss Thriller* that afternoon. Sitting in the front seat left to right were Steve Pavelko, his brother Frank—young farmers from nearby Jackson County, Minnesota—and pilot Yarns.

Yarns planned to make a loop much like Long's, heading northwest past Fort Dodge Point and then toward Dixon Beach. With *Miss Thriller* already on her way back, the boats would pass one another, Long coming in and Yarns going out, somewhere south of The Inn.

It was customary for pilots on the Okobojis to pass on the right of oncoming traffic. As Yarns neared Fort Dodge Point, he watched *Miss Thriller* coming at him in the distance on the left, just off his bow. Yarns leaned *Zipper* a little to the right to separate the boats. *Miss Thriller*, moving much faster than *Zipper*, kept pressing from the left, closing the gap between the launches. Yarns moved right again, and still the space between them narrowed. Again, Yarns leaned to the right.

The swivel-mounted headlight on *Zipper's* bow was within the pilot's reach. When the boats were about 250 yards apart, Yarns grabbed the handle on the back of the headlight and moved it left and right, waving the light side to side in the direction of *Miss Thriller* while he veered even more sharply right trying to separate the boats. The distance narrowed. Again, Yarns waved his headlight left and right at *Miss Thriller*. The faster boat kept coming hard. Just yards apart, *Miss Thriller* suddenly sped up and made a sharp left turn, cutting directly across *Zipper's* path. Yarns turned hard left and cut his engine hoping to slip behind the launch as it passed or to slow down enough to avoid reaching the faster boat. It was too late. With a terrible crash of crushing wood, *Zipper* sliced into the right rear corner of *Miss Thriller*.

The collision was as violent as it was sudden and deadly. It sheared off a section of *Miss Thriller's* transom, the flat surface forming the boat's stern, and punched a hole in *Zipper's* bow below the water line.

The impact threw *Miss Thriller* pilot Long, who was nearest the point of contact, deep between the engines. Water poured into the launches while their momentum carried them away from each other. The inrush of water at the stern of *Miss Thriller*, adding to the weight of her engines, tipped the launch vertically so quickly, it threw her passengers, who only moments before had no idea there was any danger, out of their seats and into the lake. She hung there with her bow sticking seven feet into the air and settling deeper into the water.

Long, whose foot was caught in the machinery, was pulled underwater and into a struggle for his life. Helga Hansen, who could not swim, was one of the few passengers who managed to stay in her seat as *Miss Thriller* tipped on end. She grabbed a life preserver as the rising water flushed her from the boat and into the lake with the other passengers who were screaming, crying and calling for help. They scrambled around in the dark trying to find life preservers that might have been dumped into the water. Few found any. Some managed to get back to the boat and hold on. Others grabbed onto the boat's headlights, now projecting a pair of beams straight into the sky. The beams were seen at the Central Pavilion over a mile and a half away, but no one there could know they were from a boat in trouble on the water. Others grabbed the bowline and seat backs or tried to climb onto the boat while it was rapidly settling deeper into the water.

Fifteen feet under water, Long pulled and twisted on his foot, shoe, and pant leg until he freed himself from the engines and kicked for the surface. Gasping for breath as he broke through the water, he was quickly pulled under again by passengers grasping for any kind of support. Alexander, who managed to get back to the boat after being thrown in the water, was holding onto *Miss Thriller's* bowline and trying to calm the passengers. He helped Esther Rehnstrom get a life preserver and shouted to the others to grab hold of the boat and wait for help. In their panic, however, they climbed on the boat where they could, pulling themselves up by the seat backs and deck fittings.

Their weight only hastened the boat's sinking. The fractured hull sizzled as the air inside the boat, being compressed into smaller spaces as the boat sank, seeped from the seams in her planking. *Miss Thriller* hung at the surface for only a few minutes, and then the launch slipped out from under her passengers and sank to the bottom. Her headlights still burned, illuminating the passengers from below as they thrashed and screamed in an attempt to save themselves amid a fading cone of green-yellow light. Then they flashed out, leaving the floundering passengers in the dark. Panic turned to terror. For a second time, *Miss Thriller* had sunk from beneath a boatload of passengers. This time, people would die.

In heavier-when-soaked street clothing, and many without life preservers, the 15 passengers and two pilots struggled to stay afloat in the dark. No doubt, they prayed for help. Kenneth and Roy, both good swimmers who had been teaching Neal how to swim, decided they would try for shore. Roy, who had found a life preserver, gave it to a woman who couldn't swim and didn't have one. He told her, "You need it worse than I do."[55] The boys then turned toward the lights near Fort Dodge Point, calling out to one another to stay together. When Kenneth and Roy lost contact with Neal, it frightened them and they decided to swim back to the group. Someone they thought, would hear the screaming and come to the rescue.

Since they watched *Miss Thriller* approaching, the passengers in *Zipper* had anticipated the impact but were terrified by the sound of the crash and the darkness that flashed over the boat when her lights went out. The crash had spun the launch around. She was facing back toward Arnolds Park and filling with water. Yarns passed out life preservers. "It looks bad, put these on,"[56] he told his passengers, the water already so deep he couldn't restart the engine. He encouraged the passengers to remain calm, but the two children accompanying Jessie Schneider, frightened and panicking in the dark, tried to jump out of the boat. Steve Pavelko took Patricia in his arms and Yarns grabbed Philip. They calmed the children and held them out of the water as Yarns aimed the drifting boat toward the nearest lights on shore. Behind them they could hear *Miss Thriller's* passengers in the water screaming for help, but there was nothing they could do.

Near Fort Dodge Point, 17-year-old Morris Mandelbaum of Des Moines and his sister were playing along the shore when he heard the crash and screams for help coming from across the water. Calling for his younger brother Norm to come along, the two boys rushed to the family's small outboard motorboat and headed across the water toward the shouting. With only a flashlight to help them, they raced toward the accident, passing seat cushions, life preservers and floating debris, until their light flashed across *Zipper*. Yarns and his passengers were standing in the boat, knee-deep in water, and it seemed to be sinking fast.

As the Mandelbaums pulled alongside, Yarns and Pavelko passed them the Schneider children. The men carefully moved Jessie Schneider, Jean Ellison and Naomi Adams into the motorboat. The women and children

---

[55] "NINE ARE KILLED WHEN BOATS CRASH IN OKOBOJI," *The Milford Mail*, Thursday, August 1, 1929: 8

[56] Jessie Schneider, Dickinson District Court Transcripts of Evidence Before the Grand Jury, State of Iowa vs. John and Milo Hartman, Case File 40360, RG 55 Iowa Supreme Court, State Historical Society of Iowa.

badly overloaded the small boat, and it was riding deep in the water. Morris Mandelbaum told his five new passengers to remain still. "Don't anybody sneeze,"[57] he said as he eased the boat toward The Inn, the nearest shore, almost half a mile to the north. When he arrived at the beach, the docks were filling with people who had heard the crash and had come to the waterfront to see what had happened. They helped unload the Mandelbaums' passengers, soaked but unharmed. The brothers went back out on the lake to get the others.

Lo Gipner was next to reach the *Zipper*. He had come out on the water in the *Sea Gull* to look for *Miss Thriller* because she was late returning to shore. By the time Gipner arrived, the top of *Zipper* had settled to the surface of the lake, and the Pavelko brothers, James Adams and Yarns were in water up to their chests. Gipner picked up the Pavelkos and Adams and moved off to transfer them to the bigger *Red Mahogany* that had arrived nearby. The men were taken to Arnolds Park. On shore, Frank Pavelko checked the time and found that the rising water in the boat had stopped his watch at 9:20. The next boat to reach *Zipper* found Yarns in the water behind the boat trying to push it to shore by kicking his legs. They pulled him from the water, tied onto *Zipper*, and dragged the launch to Arnolds Park. By the time the Mandelbaums returned, *Zipper* was gone. They joined the growing fleet of small boats searching the water for more victims.

Frank Hopkins of Spirit Lake, owner and pilot of the launch *Reliance*, was near The Inn with five passengers from Arnolds Park when he heard the crash. He motored through the dark in the direction of the screams and arrived about five minutes later to find *Miss Thriller* already gone and her passengers thrashing in the dark and crying for help. In his headlight, he could see *Zipper* in the distance, her passengers standing in the sinking launch as it drifted away.

Hopkins and his passengers threw their life preservers to the people in the water and tossed a rope toward a group scrambling to reach his boat. Alexander grabbed the rope and pulled himself toward *Reliance* with Lucille Patterson, Kenneth and Roy hanging onto his shoulders, holding him underwater as he went. By the time he reached the *Reliance*, he was

---

[57] Patricia Schneider Ogden in discussions with the author, July 2006.

choking and exhausted, too weak to climb aboard. Hopkins' passengers pulled him into *Reliance*. Guy Hedrick and Long, who had managed to swim to *Reliance*, pushed Kenneth, Roy, and Lucille aboard before they crawled into the boat. With nobody else left to save, Hopkins motored to Arnolds Park with the survivors.

A rowboat picked up Helga Hansen, still clinging to her life preserver, and Esther Rehnstrom, who was unconscious and being held at the surface by Mary Cummings. The women were taken to The Inn where Richard Hawley, a private airplane pilot from Fort Dodge, and Jim McCoy, a championship swimmer and diver from Des Moines who was spending the summer at The Inn teaching swimming lessons, tried in vain to revive Esther. According to Helga and Mary, she had been alive and clutching a life preserver after *Miss Thriller* went down. Bruises about her head suggested rescue boats had struck her. The rest of the passengers, Helga said, just could not stay afloat until rescue boats arrived.

The crash, more than a mile and a half north of Arnolds Park, couldn't be heard over the sounds of the amusement parks and boat traffic near shore, but word spread like wildfire when Frank Hopkins landed *Reliance* with *Miss Thriller's* survivors.

At first, people frantically searched the parks and waterfront for family and friends, any member of their party who might be missing and perhaps in one of the boats involved in the accident. Then, they flocked to the docks looking for the latest news and watched as boat after boat pulled away to join in the search. The carnival rides operated nearly empty while their merry music drifted oddly out of place across the somber, quiet crowd growing along the waterfront. The docks were so crowded with onlookers that police had to order people off so search boats could be launched and landed. *Zipper* owner John Hartman sent Milo and Let Clark out to look for his boat. By the time they arrived at the scene, *Zipper* was gone, all the survivors were out of the water, and other boats responding to the accident were using their headlights and flashlights to comb the area, searching for bodies.

Jim McCoy, unable to save Esther Rehnstrom, went out on the lake with boats from The Inn to help in the search. He dove from boat to boat in

The Death Boat

long, deep, sweeping arcs, trying to snag bodies underwater. His attempts were fruitless. A few boats lingered on the lake overnight, pulling wreckage from the water and hoping to recover bodies. Volunteers walked the shoreline along Dixon Beach and Fort Dodge Point until dawn looking for survivors or bodies that might have made it to shore. None did.

John Steinke, waiting in the crowd for his son Arnold, made frantic efforts to hire a boat after it appeared the last survivors had been brought ashore. "Give me a boat," he cried, "I'll go out and get my boy."[58] No boats were available. Every watercraft was on the water helping in the search.

In another frantic search, James and Naomi Adams, who had been taken to shore across the lake from one another, passed each other in cars several times as they traveled between Arnolds Park and The Inn looking for each other. It was hours before they met again, and by then both had come to suspect the other hadn't survived.

Mary Cummings, exhausted from searching for Lloyd and her hope seeping away, waited around the beach for hours for him to appear. Lloyd was an excellent swimmer, she assured friends, and she was sure he would make it to the park. She waited with the Steinkes at the Lakeside Store until 3 a.m., and then collapsed in grief. Her sister and friends escorted her to a cabin for the night. Small groups of people lingered along the beach at Arnolds Park all night, waiting for the latest news and possibly for survivors to be brought to shore.

As survivors arrived at Arnolds Park, one thing seemed clear: People were missing. Pete Eckman took it upon himself to find the survivors and compile a list of who was aboard the boats and who had made it back to shore. He found all the male passengers on *Zipper* had returned to the park aboard *Red Mahogany*. When the Schneider party of four and Naomi Adams were driven to Arnolds Park from their landing at The Inn, it was clear all the Eagle Boat Line boat passengers were accounted for. When Yarns was brought in with his damaged launch, it meant the

---

[58] "Sidelights Regarding the Lakes Tragedy," *The Spencer News-Herald,* Thursday, August 1, 1929: 1

missing would have been aboard *Miss Thriller.*

The *Reliance* brought in *Miss Thriller*'s pilots, so the missing were among her passengers. Eckman had seated four couples in the first two rows of the launch, but he had no idea who they were. He had boarded Henry Hintz, Lucille Patterson and John Steinke's son Arnold in the third row, and a couple of boys he didn't know were seated near local sign painter Guy Hedrick. Patterson, Hedrick, and the two boys, Kenneth and Roy, had returned with the pilots, but he couldn't find Hintz or Arnold. If Eckman hadn't seen Neal slip aboard the launch, Kenneth and Roy certainly told him their friend was on the boat and couldn't be found.

When Mary Cummings arrived at Arnolds Park still wet and frantically searching for her husband, Lloyd, Eckman learned the identity of one of the two front-row couples. Mary told Eckman two other passengers, the women who were sitting in the row behind her, came to shore in her boat. They were still at The Inn when she left to find Lloyd. One was unconscious, and volunteers were trying to revive her. Others were comforting the woman's friend.

Searching overnight, Eckman couldn't find Hintz, Arnold, Neal or Cummings, nor could he determine the names of the two women at The Inn. One had died on the dock, and the other had left The Inn and couldn't be found.

Early Monday, he was still trying to identify the six remaining passengers when Helga Hansen was located at the home of her employers, the Clintons, where she had taken refuge. She told Eckman it was her friend Esther Rehnstrom who had died Sunday night, and they had been with Milo Nelson and Thomas Christian.

At mid-morning, Eckman was still trying to identify the second couple in *Miss Thriller's* front row when someone noticed a car parked along Lake Street that hadn't been moved overnight. Authorities confirmed with a telephone call to the owner's home that it belonged to Melvin Koehnk, who had gone to the park with his sweetheart, Luella Adams. They hadn't returned home and appeared to be the other couple in *Miss Thriller's* front row. With that, Eckman had assembled a list of the 26 people who had been aboard the two launches when the accident happened. One, Esther Rehnstrom, was dead, and eight passengers, all aboard *Miss Thriller*, were missing and now presumed dead: Henry Hintz, Arnold Steinke, Neal Gelino, Lloyd Cummings, Milo Nelson, Thomas Christian, Melvin Koehnk and Luella Adams.

Chapter Seven

Recovery of the Bodies

At first light Monday morning, the work of recovering the bodies got under way. Led by Harry Tennant and Clark Albro, experienced seine fishermen, a group of volunteers in almost two dozen rowboats began dragging for bodies.

Beginning at the oil slick rising from *Miss Thriller*, the small boats worked in pairs, pulling nets hanging vertically in the water between floats on the surface and grappling hooks at the bottom. The men worked quietly to the rhythmic splash and drip of their oars as they rowed back and forth in overlapping patterns above the wreck. What few words were necessary were spoken softly and carried nearly to shore across the silent lake.

People lined Dixon Beach and the high bank north of Fort Dodge Point, watching what they could of the search going on half a mile out on the lake. As each body was snagged and brought to the surface, it was placed into one of the powerboats standing nearby and rushed to Arnolds Park. From there, it was carried from the docks to ambulances parked along the beach.

All morning a crowd had grown along the waterfront at Arnolds Park. Too far away to watch the search, they waited in small groups for news. As each powerboat left the search area and headed to shore, the crowd tightened around the docks in search of news. Behind them, the parks, which had suspended amusements during part of the search, were entertaining visitors who had come seeking a good time. The gay music and sound of people

The Death Boat

having fun seemed out of place to those aware of the sobbing family members waiting hopelessly for the recovery of their loved ones' body.

About 10:30 a.m., Tennant and Albro recovered the first body, that of the boy Neal Gelino. As his body was carried from the dock, his parents, Adelor and Myrtle Gelino, came out of the crowd rushing to the ambulance. "My poor son! My poor son!"[59] Adelor repeated as they broke down and collapsed into the arms of friends. They were led away and Neal's body was taken to a Spirit Lake funeral parlor.

All day long the scene was repeated each time a body was recovered. Tennant and Albro recovered Milo Nelson, and then Thomas Christian about noon, and then Melvin Koehnk around 1 p.m. They picked up the body of Lloyd Cummings in the afternoon, while other boats recovered the bodies of Arnold Steinke and Luella Adams. Hundreds lined the beach to watch what one reporter described as a "grim parade of the dead"[60] as the bodies came ashore. The last to be pulled from the water was Henry Hintz, his body recovered about 6:30 p.m. Monday.

The soggy street clothes, which hastened their drowning, helped in their recovery. Grappling hooks caught Henry by his coat lapel and snagged Luella's stocking. Some of the others, however, had ugly slashes made by the hooks in unsuccessful attempts to secure holds on the remains.

Luella's mother identified her daughter and Melvin Koehnk. Lloyd's sister-in-law, Ethel Heathcock, identified Lloyd's body because his wife, Mary, in her shock and grief, couldn't perform the task. The fathers of Milo and Thomas identified their sons. Monday evening, after the victims had been identified, the Dickinson County coroner, Dr. Peter G. Grimm, released a list of the dead. Not yet confident in Pete Eckman's list, he told reporters as many as three more bodies might be trapped in *Miss Thriller's* hull. The bodies were taken to funeral parlors in Spirit Lake or sent to establishments near their homes to be mourned and buried.

---

[59] "Boat Tragedy Brings Arrests," *Des Moines (Iowa) Tribune-Capital,* Tuesday, July 30, 1929: 2
[60] "Nine Are Dead In Boat Crash," *The Des Moines Register,* Tuesday, July 30, 1929: 3

Chapter Eight

The Funerals

On Wednesday, July 31, in homes and churches across five northwest Iowa counties and a small village in southern Minnesota, families began burying their spouses and children, their promising young people and successful businessmen.

In Buena Vista County, mourners gathered at Immanuel Lutheran Church in Elk Township to remember Esther Rehnstrom. The little church where she attended services and Sunday school was too small to accommodate all those who came to say goodbye. Those unable to get inside gathered around the front door to listen to the eulogy and comfort the family as they emerged after the service. Rehnstrom, a graduate of Highview Consolidated School, five miles west of Rembrandt, Iowa, and Mankato Commercial College in Mankato, Minnesota, had moved to Arnolds Park to take a position at the post office only six weeks before the accident. Following her funeral service, 22-year-old Esther Anna Evelyn Rehnstrom was buried in the Scandinavian Cemetery north of Alta, Iowa. She left behind her parents, Edward and Anna Rehnstrom, and seven siblings.

At 1:30 that afternoon at Grace Methodist Episcopal Church in nearby Spencer, the Rev. Herbert Clegg began the first of two services for the victims. First came a double funeral for Melvin Koehnk and Luella Adams. Because Melvin and Luella had been dating for more than a year and met their deaths together, their parents considered a double funeral appropriate. Melvin, who was 22, was the oldest of Otto and Anna Koehnk's eight children. He farmed with his dad and, for the past two years, had driven the Everly, Iowa, school bus. Dozens of schoolchildren had gathered at his parents' home when they learned of the accident, and many were there for the service. Melvin Thomas Koehnk was buried in the Lone Tree Cemetery, southwest of Everly.

Luella Veda Adams was just 17. She had graduated from the eighth grade in the spring of 1927 and had been living with her parents, Earle and Celia Adams, and her older brother, Harold, at the time of the accident. Luella was buried in the Pleasant View Cemetery in Hartley, Iowa.

As the Rev. Clegg concluded the first funeral, the family and friends of the youngest victim, Neal Gelino, began to arrive. Earlier, the Rev. Robert T. Chipperfield, pastor of the Methodist Episcopal Church in Estherville, Iowa, had conducted a service at the Gelino home in Estherville for friends of the family. Neal's schoolmates gathered in the yard to comfort one another. His body then was taken to Grace Methodist in Spencer, where the Rev. Clegg conducted his funeral at 2:30 p.m. Neal was born in Spencer and still had family there, where his father, an award-winning cook, had operated a small restaurant. During the next few years, Adelor Gelino owned a series of restaurants in southwestern Minnesota and northwestern Iowa. By the time Neal was in the third grade, Gelino had moved his family to Estherville, where he owned the Gelino Café. In April 1929, Gelino sold his Estherville cafe and his newer restaurant, Violet's Eat Shoppe in Milford and moved to Arnolds Park. There, he took over operation of a hamburger stand at one of the amusement parks. Neal joined him there when school was dismissed for the summer, while his mother and sisters remained in Estherville. Neal, a confident student and likable boy, spent his days around the amusement parks making friends with the concessioners and locals. He quickly befriended Jap Alexander, who allowed him to ride free in empty seats aboard *Miss Thriller*. Their friendship had put him aboard *Miss Thriller* the night of the accident. Neal Burdett Gelino, the middle child and only son of Adelor and Myrtle Gelino, was buried in Riverside Cemetery in Spencer.

Two churches in Osceola County in northwest Iowa held funerals that afternoon. At the Methodist Church in Harris, mourners said goodbye to one of the town's most prominent and successful businessmen, Henry

Hintz. He had been the superintendent at Dry Lake Farm, a 400-acre operation south of town. Owned by the state and farmed by trustees from the state penitentiary at Fort Madison, the farm provided potatoes to Iowa's state institutions. At 50, Henry was the oldest victim of the crash. He left behind his wife, Laura; two grown daughters, Verna and Alma; a teenage son, Neill; and three grandchildren. Henry Hintz was buried in the Ocheyedan Township Cemetery west of Ocheyedan, Iowa, about 25 miles straight west of Okoboji.

At the same time, 10 miles south of Ocheyedan in May City, services for Arnold Steinke were held at St. John Lutheran Church. Earlier private prayers had been offered at the family's home. Arnold, the only son of John and Gustie Steinke, was 16 years old. He had a younger sister, Helen. Arnold John Henry Steinke was buried in the Harrison Cemetery southeast of May City.

Wednesday's seventh funeral was for Lloyd Cummings, the only victim not from Iowa. His body was taken from Spirit Lake to the home of his mother and stepfather, Alma and George Simning, in Wabasso, Minnesota, just more than 60 miles straight north of Okoboji. Lloyd owned and operated a restaurant adjacent to the pool hall run by his stepfather in the Deutscher Bier Garten building in Wabasso. Simning owned the building. Services began with private prayers at his parents' home and concluded with a funeral at the English Evangelical Lutheran Church. His mother, Alma, and his wife, Mary, accompanied his body, which was taken by train, to Princeton, Ill. Lloyd Frederick Cummings was buried Friday, August 2, among his family in the Oakland Cemetery in Princeton.

On Thursday, August 1, friends Milo Nelson and Thomas Christian were remembered in a double funeral in Linn Grove, Iowa. Before the funeral, the Rev. Knut G. Hatlen of the First Lutheran Church of Sioux Rapids, Iowa, conducted private prayers for Milo at his parents' home, while the Rev. Theodore Lerud of the Little Sioux Church near Rembrandt, Iowa, conducted prayers for Thomas at his parents' home. Mourners then walked from their homes to the south end of Main Street where they joined to form a double file that proceeded two blocks east to the Linn Grove Lutheran Church. Almost 1,000 people, three times the population of Linn Grove, attended the funeral. Only a fraction of the mourners could fit into the church. People outside followed the services through the open door and windows. Nelson, who was 25, was the oldest son of Perry and Matilda Nelson, who had five children. Christian was 21 years old, the second son of Carl and Mary Christian's six children. Elmore Milo Nelson and Thomas LeRoy Christian were buried across the street from the church in the Barnes Township Cemetery.

Chapter Nine

News Coverage of the Accident

Radio stations spread the news of the crash across Iowa overnight. By Monday morning, everyone in the state had been given the opportunity to hear about the accident, but the reports contained few details.

Monday morning's *Des Moines Register*, Iowa's largest daily newspaper, incorrectly reported two steamboats had collided and that most of those aboard were children. Monday's *Sioux City Journal* said one girl drowned and a 17-year-old boy was unaccounted for as a result of the collision of two speedboats. A United Press news service dispatch at daybreak said dragging for bodies was underway, but "efforts to determine the dead and missing is almost purely guesswork."[61]

While the information reaching the news desks was sketchy, it was clear many people were missing and perhaps dead, and editors scrambled to get reporters to the scene. *The Des Moines Register* dispatched its airplane *Good News* at first light Monday morning. Aboard the five-seat airplane were city editor Richard L. Wilson, correspondent C.C. Clifton, and news photographer George Yates. Also onboard was Cliff Millen, a reporter for the *Register's* sister newspaper, the afternoon Des Moines *Capital-Tribune*.

The Associated Press sent Theodore F. Koop to the scene from Des Moines, and the *World-Herald* dispatched Allan Kohan in a private plane

---

[61] "10 Dead, 4 Missing and 31 Injured, Toll of Weekend in Iowa," *Waterloo (Iowa) Evening Courier*, Monday, July 29, 1929: 2

from Omaha, Nebraska. Raymond Olson, a reporter for *The Sioux City Tribune*, rushed to the scene by automobile.

Just before 9 a.m., pilot Charley Gatschet landed the ironically named *Good News* north of Milford on the same stubble field used by Lo Gipner when he was flying for the Milford Aero Club. Milford wouldn't build an airfield until 1930. Kohan's plane followed him minutes later. The newsmen rushed to Arnolds Park and fanned out across the lakefront looking for the pilots, survivors and the officials who were trying to determine the number and identity of the victims. They described the search for the bodies and the attempts to locate *Miss Thriller,* and looked for the cause of the accident. The first report from the newspapermen on the scene appeared in Monday afternoon's *Capital-Tribune*, where Millen listed nine names—five dead and four missing. Several of the names were misspelled and most on the list didn't include their ages, but he was able to report that the bodies of Koehnk, Rehnstrom and Gelino had been recovered.

He also told the story of Morris and Norm Mandelbaum, who had rescued five passengers from the *Zippe*r, and Jim McCoy, who had tried to help Esther Rehnstrom and later joined the search for the bodies.

Koop's first reports for The Associated Press also appeared in Monday afternoon newspapers. *Miss Thriller* was a "reconstructed government-built submarine chaser,"[62] he wrote, and she was reported to be the fastest passenger boat in the country.

Wilson, Kohan, and Olson's first stories wouldn't appear until Tuesday's newspapers, the same day that Koop's updated accounts appeared in the *Watertown (NY) Standard* under stacked headlines that read "*Miss Thriller*, Widely Known Along River, Carries Thrill Seekers to Death" and "Built for Claude Ellis,"[63] and *The New York Times* carried Koop's account on the bottom of Page 16 with the headline "Nine Dead, 3 Missing in Speedboat Crash."[64] Koop also reported that one of the heroes of the crash was 9-

---

[62] "9 DEAD, 3 MISSING IN BOAT CRASH," *The Burlington (Iowa) Hawk-Eye*, Tuesday, July 30, 1929: 1
[63] "*Miss Thriller*, Widely Known Along River, Carries Thrill Seekers to Death," *Watertown Standard*, Tuesday, July 30, 1929: 1
[64] "NINE DEAD, 3 MISSING IN SPEEDBOAT CRASH," *The New York Times,* Tuesday, July 30, 1929: 16

year-old Roy Barnes, who had given his life preserver to a woman without one and apparently unable to swim. It would be several days before officials would learn that the woman was Lucille Patterson. At least two newspapers compared the loss of life in the accident to the Spirit Lake Massacre.

Photographer Yates made pictures of the fleet of rowboats dragging the lake, the crowd gathered around the docks at Arnolds Park and the victims' covered bodies as they were brought to shore. He took photographs of the damage to *Zipper*, now pulled up on shore, along with the pilots, survivors and the Mandelbaums as Morris told his story to reporters.

Zipper, a gaping hole in her prow, rests on the beach after the accident.
Courtesy of the Iowa Great Lakes Maritime Museum

Yates' photographs were flown back to Des Moines aboard the *Good News* and appeared in Tuesday morning's *Register* and Tuesday afternoon's *Capital-Tribune*. The *Register* shared Yates' photographs with weekly newspapers, which printed them the following Thursday. Raymond Olson's first pictures wouldn't appear in *The Sioux City Tribune* until Wednesday and in the *Spencer News-Herald* on Thursday.

Coroner Grimm, who hadn't been contacted Sunday night, arrived at the docks Monday morning. Working from Pete Eckman's list, he began matching the bodies as they were recovered with the known missing. Boat Inspector Thompson, who wasn't at the scene Sunday night either, gathered what information he could, telegraphed a report to Governor Hammill and asked for instructions. The governor wired back: "Allow no boats to be operated by offenders in Sunday night's accident until the cause is ascertained and the responsibility fixed. Revoke all licenses of reckless

The Death Boat

drivers. Vigorous action at Arnolds Park is essential."[65]

Thompson called in the Eagle Boat Line launches, removing them from the search for bodies. Roy Lombard, who had pulled his boats off the water and out of the horde of boats on the lake, sent the *Sea Gull* back into the search. Late Monday afternoon, Hammill initiated a state investigation into the accident, dispatching to the Lakes Murray L. Hutton, superintendent of state parks, along with Oscar Mead, state agent, and W.E.G. Saunders, chairman of the state conservation board. Already on the lakefront and conducting his own investigation was Dickinson County State's Attorney Kenneth B. Welty.

Late Sunday night, as the search for the missing was under way, wild speculation spread about the accident's cause. When it became clear that *Zipper* struck *Miss Thriller,* blame quickly focused on *Zipper* pilot Harold Yarns. "Yarnes [*sic*] was a green driver," Pete Eckman said. "There was no doubt he was probably blinded by *Miss Thriller's* headlights."[66] Some questioned Yarns' eyesight because he wore heavy glasses. Others speculated he must have been trying to give his passengers a thrill by crossing behind *Miss Thriller* for a splashing and got too close.

Zipper owner John Hartman took a different view. He said one of *Miss Thriller's* engines must have ceased to function, throwing the launch in front of *Zipper,* or that pilot Frank Long, new to *Miss Thriller,* might have thrown the wrong throttle trying to avoid the crash and turned into *Zipper's* path. Newspapermen working the story Monday didn't take long to uncover the ongoing dock war between the Hartmans and the operators of *Miss Thriller.* By that afternoon, stories blaming the accident on the competition between the boatmen began appearing in newspapers across the country.

Monday afternoon, after the recovery of Henry Hintz's body, Coroner Grimm met briefly with reporters. After releasing the victims' names and telling reporters as many as three bodies might still be trapped in the boat, he said he was inclined to believe *Zipper's* pilot was responsible for the accident, given the fact that it struck *Miss Thriller,* but the final

---

[65] "Boatmen Are Arrested on 2nd Degree Murder Counts: Inquest Held," *The Spencer Reporter,* Wednesday, July 31, 1929: 1

[66] "Sidelights Regarding the Lakes Tragedy," *The Spencer News-Herald,* Thursday, August 1, 1929: 1

determination would have to wait until the inquest. That would be held as soon as state investigators arrived.

County Attorney Welty agreed with the coroner's understanding of the accident, but he also had personal knowledge of the intense feud between the Hartmans and the operators of *Miss Thriller*. "My inquiry among the witnesses and survivors tends to indicate criminal negligence,"[67] he told reporters. "Hartman threatened to get them and he did get them."[68]

Monday night, Welty telephoned the governor with his findings, and Hammill instructed Welty to have the pilot and owners of *Zipper* arrested and charged with second-degree murder. None of the men could be found Monday night. Sheriff George Paulson arrested the men Tuesday morning, and just after 10 a.m. they appeared before Justice of the Peace Charles W. Price. They were arraigned, pleaded not guilty, and released on $5,000 bond each. Marcus Snyder, president of the First National Bank in Spirit Lake, put up the money for the Hartmans, while Bert Yarns paid for the release of his son Harold.

With reporters already at the courthouse, news of the arrests reached the daily newspaper offices almost immediately, and extra editions were printed and rushed to the Lakes. A chartered airplane carrying *The Des Moines Register's* extra edition arrived at noon. Area residents were reading the story of the arraignment of the Hartmans and Yarns within two hours of the arrests. In Spencer, newsboys were selling *The Sioux City Tribune's* extra on the streets before 6 p.m. Later, *The Spencer Reporter* bragged to its readers that it beat the *Tribune* to the story because hundreds of people had read the report of the arrests posted on the *Reporter*'s office windows two hours before the *Tribune*'s special edition arrived in town.

At 2 p.m. Tuesday, Coroner Grimm, convened the inquest into the sinking of *Miss Thriller*. It was his second inquest into a fatal boating accident on West Lake Okoboji in four years.

In July 1926, Grimm conducted an inquiry into the death of 67-year-old

---

[67] "NINE DROWNED IN LAKE OKOBOJI SPEEDBOAT CRASH," *The Omaha (NE) World Herald*, Tuesday, July 30, 1929: 2
[68] "THREATS BY ZIPPER OWNERS CHARGED," *Mitchell (SD) Evening Republican*, Thursday, August 1, 1929: 1

Urvin Meyerdirk, who was fishing from a rowboat at sunset when his boat was run over by the speedboat *Dundee* driven by Gail Parker, Charles Parker's grandson. The accident severed Meyerdirk's right leg. He died a few hours later. Gail Parker testified the sun's glare and its reflection on the water had prevented him from seeing Meyerdirk's boat. The coroner's jury found that no crime had been committed. Meyerdirk was former *Miss Thriller* owner Let Clark's father-in-law.

More than 300 spectators, many of them relatives and friends of the dead, filled the third-floor courtroom of the Dickinson County Courthouse for the *Miss Thriller* inquest. Grimm's three-member jury included the superintendent of schools, an insurance salesman, and the pastor of the Presbyterian Church of Spirit Lake. The state's investigators were seated near the witness stand and nearby sat Governor Hammill's personal representative, friend and former Judge Charles S. Bradshaw.

The courtroom was sweltering. The previous week's heat had returned. The tan brick courthouse baked under the afternoon sun, with temperatures in the mid-90s. It felt as though all the heat had collected in the third-floor courtroom. What breeze there was couldn't seem to find its way into the east- and west-facing windows. Some men shed their coats and others stripped to their undershirts in the stifling heat.

Grimm, dressed in an immaculate white suit appropriate for the heat of the day, began by releasing a revised list of the victims and told the court he was confident no bodies remained trapped in *Miss Thriller*. He called the first witness, pilot Harold Yarns. As Yarns walked to the stand, his attorney, Walter B. Bedell, asked the court to excuse the young man on the grounds he was under arrest on a charge of second-degree murder and his testimony might be self-incriminating. Yarns was excused. As he left the stand, a piece of *Miss Thriller's* transom, recovered from the water Sunday night, was hauled into the courtroom from a private stairway behind the judge's bench. It was placed in the front of the room as evidence of the accident.

Jap Alexander was called as the next witness. Responding to questions, he told the jury he was the mechanic aboard *Miss Thriller* on Sunday, and he and Frank Long were having their best day ever. Just after dark, they left on their normal loop around the lake, headed first toward The Inn, west toward The Manhattan and then back to Arnolds Park. They had made their last turn at The Manhattan and were returning to Arnolds Park when *Zipper* hit and sank them.

Zipper pilot Harold Yarns
Courtesy of the Iowa Great Lakes Maritime Museum

Alexander described *Miss Thriller's* sudden tip bow up in the water, the struggle to find life preservers, the panicking passengers' scramble to climb on the boat that hastened her sinking, and his rescue by *Reliance*.

"Did you try to get out of the way?" Grimm asked. [69] "Yes, we speeded up our boat so as to get out of the way or it would have hit us practically in the center," Alexander replied. [70]

Alexander was questioned by jurors Fred Dowden, the insurance agent; School Superintendent Harry Ilsley; and the Rev. Herbert Marsh. He had acted as the boat's lookout and said he first noticed the *Zipper's* light about half a mile away and perhaps 300 feet off to the right. The boat appeared to be going toward Miller's Bay. "Didn't you consider this light was a hazard when you saw it first a half mile off?" Dowden asked.[71] "Not while the light was pointing in the opposite direction," replied Alexander. "I didn't pay any more attention to it. The first thing we knew he's yards from us, hit us and knocked the back end of our boat off."[72]

After a few follow-up questions about who had the fastest boat on the

---

[69] "Evidence at the Coroner's Inquest: A complete transcript," *The Spencer News-Herald*, Thursday, August 8, 1929: 10
[70] Ibid.
[71] Ibid.
[72] Ibid.

The Death Boat

lake—Alexander said he thought it was *Miss Thriller*—and how fast they were traveling Sunday night, "between 25 and 35 miles an hour,"[73] he was dismissed. Frank Long then was called to the stand.

Long also described accelerating at the last minute to avoid the crash. He told the court he had been trapped in the engines and pulled underwater when the stern went down, and had reached the surface only to be pulled under by panicked passengers. He was rescued by Frank Hopkins on the *Reliance*. Long testified that he first noticed *Zipper* far off and to the right and coming toward him in a zigzagging course. The course was so confusing he didn't know which direction *Zipper* was going, he said. The boat's light was not pointing straight ahead but off to one side of the launch, giving the impression the boat was going in another direction.

Long said he had slowed down *Miss Thriller*, and when he saw they were going to be hit, he opened up the throttles to gain headway. "I tried to keep from going toward him," he said, but the other craft "seemed to cut towards us and we were struck."[74] He said he was entirely innocent of any fault in the crash. No one asked him who should be blamed.

Long's testimony was followed by most of the survivors aboard *Miss Thriller*, including Roy Barnes. He startled the courtroom when he volunteered, "It looked like the *Zipper* tried to hit us."[75] After four hours of testimony and almost a dozen witnesses, the inquest was adjourned. The wilted spectators cleared the courtroom seeking relief from the heat on the courthouse lawn, where they waited for the inquiry's verdict. Two hours later, Grimm reconvened the inquest. His jury wanted to hear from Inspector Thompson.

On the stand, Thompson identified himself as the state boating inspector, a position he had held for 32 years. Thompson said the governor appoints the inspector, whose job is to license boats and pilots, and enforce boating regulations. He had inspected *Zipper* about June 1 and *Miss Thriller* about July 1, Thompson told the jury, and each was in perfect order. The boats were safe, had the required safety equipment, and neither boat was

---

[73] Ibid.
[74] "Evidence at the Coroner's Inquest: A complete transcript," *The Spencer News-Herald*, Thursday, August 8, 1929: 11
[75] Ibid.

overloaded the night of the accident. Long and Alexander, he continued, had been pilots for more than 10 years, and on July 26 he had licensed Yarns, who was new to West Lake Okoboji but had considerable experience operating boats on Big Spirit Lake.

"Is it true that the *Thriller* has sunk once this year?"[76] the jury asked. "No, *Miss Thriller* did not sink this year,"[77] he replied, and he went on to say he had "tied it up"[78] last season because she was in bad shape, and he did not permit the launch to operate again until repairs were made. He had monitored the repairs made by Long and Alexander, Thompson said, before licensing her to return to service.

"Your conclusion about the condition of the boat was not determined by the fact that one of the pilots was your son-in-law?" a juror asked.[79] "Not a particle," snapped Thompson, whose daughter Genevieve was married to Frank Long.[80]

One of the jurors asked Thompson about lights on motor launches: "Is it the law that they shall have two headlights?"[81] "No, sir, the law says you shall have one headlight."[82] "Is the light to be swiveling or stationary?" the juror continued. "Either one," answered Thompson, "but it must be there."[83] He testified, without citing a source, that a speed limit of 30 miles an hour existed on the lake and that it was customary for pilots to maintain 100 feet from one another as they traveled the lakes. In all cases, he continued, when approaching another boat, pilots were to pass on the right. "It's a government rule…it has been followed and been the custom ever since I can remember," said Thompson.[84]

Had there been any complaints about these boats getting too close to each other? "No, there hasn't," replied Thompson.[85] Did he recall any instance

---

[76] Ibid.
[77] "Evidence at the Coroner's Inquest: A complete transcript," *The Spencer News-Herald,* Thursday, August 8, 1929: 11
[78] Ibid.
[79] Ibid.
[80] Ibid.
[81] Ibid.
[82] Ibid.
[83] Ibid.
[84] Ibid.
[85] Ibid.

where either boat line would be open to censure for its conduct? "I have never seen any myself this year," Thompson answered.[86] Finally, the jury asked Thompson if he had formed an opinion as to which if any of the pilots might be negligent. "Yes, I have," replied Thompson, and then he hesitated. "Is it necessary for me to answer that?"[87]

"I am asking you, Mr. Thompson, because you as state inspector have had years of experience in this work and you know the nature of the accident and the way the boats collided, and you must have formed an opinion and that opinion might have some value to us in arriving at our conclusion," a juror pushed.[88]

Without naming Yarns, Thompson replied, "Well, from the fact that the sled had gone by this other boat and that he (Yarns) struck them way back here (referring to the back of the launch), I don't see how any reasonable person could figure that these men (Long and Alexander) were in the wrong." There must have been a mechanical problem with *Zipper* or the new pilot "lost his head," Thompson said.[89]

After almost two hours on the stand, the inspector was excused. The jury deliberated but a few minutes and announced its verdict just before 10 p.m. The passengers had come to their death because of the "carelessness of the drivers of *Miss Thriller* and the owners and pilot of the *Zipper*."[90]

The public didn't receive the news well: Nine people were dead, and the inquest blamed it on carelessness. The *Sibley (Iowa) Gazette*, wrote, "Someone is responsible for the wholesale slaughter of human life and somebody should pay the penalty."[91] The *Estherville (Iowa) Enterprise*, went further saying, "Hanging is too d--- good for those who are guilty...Let there be no whitewash...in this case."[92] The *Sioux City Tribune* wasn't impressed either. "The tragedy was so needless that the lake residents are

---

[86] Ibid.
[87] Ibid.
[88] Ibid.
[89] Ibid.
[90] "Coroner Jury – Carelessness of Pilots and Managers," *Spirit Lake Beacon*, Thursday, August 1, 1929: 1
[91] "Action is Demanded In Probe," *The Milford Mail*, Thursday, August 15, 1929: 5
[92] "Three Charged With Second Degree Murder in Boat Crash," *The Estherville (Iowa) Enterprise*, Wednesday, July 31, 1929: 1

righteously up in arms," the editor wrote. "Investigation! Bah!"[93]

Grimm later explained the verdict to a reporter for *The Milford Mail*. *Zipper's* owners and Yarns were guilty of carelessness because they failed to have two pilots as the law required when passengers might obstruct the pilot's view, as Thompson had testified. *Miss Thriller's* pilots were careless because they both testified they saw the light of *Zipper* approximately one-half mile off and didn't keep an eye on the boat. Whether their carelessness constituted criminal negligence wasn't for his jury to decide, Grimm said.

Welty, too was disappointed, saying "I consider the jury's report unreasonable and unjust in view of the evidence."[94] Given the rivalry on the lakefront and the pressure the Hartmans had brought to bear on *Miss Thriller's* operators, he suspected Yarns had been instructed to interfere with the other boat's operations, resulting in an accident. He intended to proceed with second-degree murder charges.

By the time the coroner's verdict was printed in the newspapers, Justice Price had set the preliminary hearing for the second-degree murder charge against Harold Yarns for 9 a.m. Thursday. Almost 400 people tried to get into the courtroom. The crowd spilled out of the courtroom's double doors onto the third-floor landing and down the wide wooden staircase to the floor below.

First on the stand was pilot Long. He was followed by Alexander and *Miss Thriller's* passengers, including Helga Hansen. She had left the funeral of Milo Nelson and Thomas Christian early to testify. Long testified the first time he saw *Zipper* she was to his left, only 100 feet from his boat. He tried to spurt out of the way but was hit. He also said *Zipper* had not been holding a steady course, and her headlight was not shining forward but at an angle, suggesting she was not coming toward his boat.

Under cross-examination, Long said there were 14 life preservers aboard his boat and seven flotation cushions that padded the wooden bench seats. He revealed his pilot's license had lapsed five years ago and that Inspector Thompson granted him a new one without the prescribed examination. He

---

[93] "NO WHITEWASH IN THIS CASE," *Spencer News-Herald,* Thursday, August 8, 1929: 14
[94] "BLAME PLACED ON BOAT MEN IN LAKE ACCIDENT," *The Sioux City (Iowa) Tribune,* Wednesday, July 31, 1929: 1

The Death Boat

also said no one seemed to follow any navigational rules on Lake Okoboji.

Inspector Thompson, who was on the stand when court adjourned Thursday afternoon, testified that he had never, until that week, seen a copy of the conservation board's rules regarding speed limits on Iowa lakes nor did he know that swivel lights were required on all boats.

But the real clash in the hearing Thursday was between County Attorney Welty, who was 28 years old and, according to *The Sioux City Journal*, probably the youngest state's attorney in Iowa, and defense attorneys Harry Narey and Walter Bedell. They were two of the best-known attorneys in northwest Iowa. They filled the courtroom with personal attacks and heated outbursts that turned the hearing into a courtroom equivalent of the waterfront warfare at Arnolds Park.

Beginning with the first witness, Welty implied the rivalry on the lakefront contributed to the accident. As he had told reporters the day before, "Hartman threatened to get them and he did get them."[95] Narey denied any such threats had been made and dismissed Welty's accusations telling the court, "There is nothing to that at all. I don't think for a minute that this rag chewing quarrel between the boatmen had a single thing to do with the tragedy." He continued, "I can't believe that either pilot had any intention to cause a collision."[96]

Narey then came at Welty, charging that the new county attorney was mishandling the investigation (Welty was elected in November 1928 and had been in office only since January). Welty, he said, should have taken the matter before the grand jury for a complete examination of the evidence before any charges were filed.

Welty responded that the attorneys for the Eagle Boat Line were preventing a thorough accident examination. The witnesses, he told the court, weren't testifying freely and honestly. Narey admitted he had told his clients to "keep their mouths shut,"[97] and then came at the county attorney again.

---

[95] "WELTY CHARGES ZIPPER OWNERS WITH THREAT TO 'GET' 'THRILLER'", *Daily Argus-Leader (Sioux Falls, SD)*, Thursday, August, 1, 1929: 2
[96] "Pilot of Zipper Freed of Murder," *The Spencer News-Herald,* Thursday, August 8, 1929: 13
[97] "Charge Laxity in Probe Of Okoboji Boat Tragedy," *The Sioux City Tribune,* Friday, August 2, 1929: 4

Welty, he said, was partial in this matter. He had represented the owners of *Miss Thriller* before the state conservation board, and now he was conducting a one-sided investigation to protect her pilots. The coroner's jury had found the operators of both boats guilty of carelessness, Narey continued, but Welty had filed charges against only *Zipper*'s pilot and owners.

A frustrated Welty turned to the audience and appealed for help. Could anyone in the courtroom, he asked, provide firsthand information that could help determine who was responsible for the accident? At that, Narey sprang to his feet shouting: "The county attorney has never sought information from us after he filed this dastardly charge of second-degree murder. There is ample evidence to show that the *Thriller* might have been to blame."[98] Some in the audience broke out in applause. Justice Price demanded order in the court, and when Welty finished his examination of Inspector Thompson, adjourned for the day.

By the time court was adjourned, conservation board chairman Saunders had heard enough about the rivalry between the passenger boat operators. He told reporters, "I think the solution of the whole matter would be a publicly owned dock under rigid supervision." He said he would recommend the board adopt stringent new boating regulations across the state.[99]

Narey's cross-examination of Thompson on Friday morning further fanned the hot tempers. He led Thompson through testimony that revealed *Miss Thriller* had sunk at her dock a year earlier, and on another occasion she had filled with water while out on the lake and had to be towed to shore. She "had been patched" up after that, snapped Thompson, and she was seaworthy. If not, she would not have been licensed.[100]

Next, Narey introduced the photograph of *Miss Thriller* sunk at her dock. Welty sprang to his feet with a loud objection. The photo, he protested, had been used by the Hartmans to smear the boat after John Hartman had it swamped. It was not evidence that *Miss Thriller* was unseaworthy but proof

---

[98] "Pilot of Zipper Freed of Murder," *The Spencer News-Herald,* Thursday, August 8, 1929: 13
[99] "CHARGES TIEUP IN BOAT PROBE," *The Des Moines Register,* Friday, August 2, 1929: 4
[100] "Pilot of Zipper Freed of Murder," *The Spencer News-Herald,* Thursday, August 8, 1929: 13

the Hartmans were out to "get" *Miss Thriller*.

Finally, Narey called pilot Lo Gipner. He testified that *Miss Thriller* had sunk in the St. Lawrence River before she was brought to Okoboji. Narey concluded, "*Miss Thriller* was not a fit boat to be riding the waves of Lake Okoboji and the boat inspector and the board of conservation should not have let it go out."[101] Welty protested, saying *Miss Thriller* was safe, her seaworthiness was not the cause of the accident, and Narey was creating hard feelings about the boat. At that, attorney Bedell came to his feet saying: "If there is any animosity in this case, it surely exists in the office of the county attorney. He has handled the investigation with one thing in mind and that is 'getting' Hartman..."[102]

Justice Price had had enough and gave the attorneys what *The (Dubuque) Telegraph-Herald* called a bawling out. "I am the sole authority in the court and my ruling will stand; from now on we are going to cut out a lot of the playing around," said Price, addressing Welty, Narey, and Bedell, who was Price's son-in-law.[103] But the sparring between the attorneys continued through closing arguments. Narey finished with, "If there was any carelessness in this collision, it was on the part of the operators of *Miss Thriller* rather than the *Zipper*."[104] He moved for a dismissal. After considerable argument from Welty, Price sustained the motion and dismissed the case. Yarns never took the stand.

In handing down his decision, Justice Price said it was the first time in his 21 years of service that he felt compelled to explain his action. "Two things appeared from the testimony," he said. "If there was any light on the *Zipper*, it was not in such shape as to be visible to the occupants of *Miss Thriller*. It also appears that *Miss Thriller* was not following instructions for boats on the lake and turned to the left (in front of *Zipper*). Altho [*sic*] it seems that somebody made a mistake, all I can do is to turn Harold Yarnes [*sic*]

---

[101] "Okoboji Boat Pilot is Freed of Charges," *Mason City (Iowa) Globe-Gazette*, Friday, August 2, 1929: 2
[102] Ibid.
[103] "Charge Laxity in Probe Of Okoboji Boat Tragedy," *The Sioux City Tribune*, Friday, August 2, 1929: 4
[104] "Boat Skipper Free; Lawyers "Bawled Out" *The (Dubuque) Telegraph-Herald*, Friday, August 2, 1929: 1

loose."[105] Court adjourned at noon.

As he left the courtroom, a stunned Welty refused to say whether he would drop the charges against John and Milo Hartman scheduled at 2 o'clock that afternoon. Then, moments before the hearings were to begin, he had them dismissed. He told the press Yarns' dismissal wasn't an acquittal. He was dropping the charges against the Hartmans and taking the case before a grand jury. Welty's investigation to determine whether rivalry between the owners of *Zipper* and the pilots of *Miss Thriller* contributed to the accident would continue.

---

[105] "OKOBOJI BOAT PILOT IS FREED." *Mason City Globe-Gazette,* Friday, August 2, 1929: 1

The Death Boat

Chapter Ten

Governor Hammill Steps In

News of the dismissal flashed across the state and re-inflamed the public's disappointment over the outcome of the coroner's inquest. Editors from across the region began pressing the state to find answers and hold the guilty accountable. Some were upset Yarns was never put on the stand; others asked if the state was even concerned with getting to the truth. The *Omaha World-Herald* wanted to know if people's lives were being put in jeopardy just to satisfy private grudges or so one rival could "show the other up."[106] The *Estherville Enterprise* said, "It's time the state took hold of these matters and at once."[107] *The Lake Park News* added that, "It is the duty of the people of this territory and the state officials to see that justice is meted out to all of the guilty." [108]

The governor's office was flooded with telegrams demanding action and justice for the victims. On Saturday, six days after the crash, Governor Hammill went to Spirit Lake to conduct a personal investigation. He met with Hutton, Mead and Saunders, who had been attending hearings, interviewing officials and lakefront business owners, and inspecting the waterfront at Arnolds Park. He drew up new state boating rules. They

---

[106] "Get the Truth at Okoboji," *Spirit Lake Beacon*, Thursday, August 15, 1929: 8
[107] "Editors Demand "No Whitewash," *The Spencer News-Herald,* Thursday, August 8, 1929:14
[108] "NINE LOSE LIVES IN OKOBOJI BOAT DISASTER," *The Lake Park (Iowa) News*, Thursday, August 1, 1929: 1

The Death Boat

included a speed limit of 20 miles an hour on Iowa lakes, slower when approaching and departing shore, and barred passenger boats from the water from sunset to sunrise. Hammill put Mead in charge of boating on all Iowa lakes.

Before he left on Sunday, he revoked the pilot licenses of Yarns, Long, and Alexander and released the Eagle Boat Line launches. John Hartman had been threatening Thompson with legal action if the inspector didn't let him operate his boats. Under the new rules, the Eagle Boat Line boats were back at their docks at sundown each evening. By Wednesday, signs with the new regulations and speed limits were posted along the waterfront at Arnold Park.

While much of the state seemed relieved Hammill had taken a hand in the situation, people at Arnolds Park who knew the Lakes took a much different view. The rules would be a heavy blow to speedboat operators such as John Hartman, Roy Lombard, and Frank Hopkins. Most of their passengers were young people seeking fast, thrilling rides across the lake. The speed limit threatened their ridership, and businesses and tourism to the Lakes in general. Banning all passenger boats at night seemed excessive. Not only did it put a stop to night speedboat rides, it also meant the end of the popular steamboat cruises in the moonlight and evening passage from Arnolds Park to the ballrooms around the lake. And the new regulations had not addressed the rivalry between the boat operators.

The day after the new regulations were posted, Leslie E. Francis, the former senator who had been at Okoboji the night of the accident and attended the court hearings, sent a letter to the governor challenging the rules and suggesting a more appropriate response to the accident. The letter was reprinted in newspapers across the state. It began, "It is evident these rules were prepared by someone just enough acquainted with the Lakes to know exactly what is required to destroy the boat business absolutely."[109] He asked, "Why all this fuss about speed?"[110] The truth of the matter, he pointed out, is that speed was not the cause of the accident, and he questioned the need for banning passenger boats after dark. The former senator proposed regulations that included frequent inspections of

---

[109] "BOATS ON THE LAKES," *The Des Moines Register*, August 12, 1929: 4
[110] Ibid.

passenger boats, annual examinations of pilots and engineers, and a requirement that all boats be bonded. The bonding companies, he said, would protect the public by their examination of the boats and operators. Francis also proposed boats be required to carry "two lights of different color at either side near the bow" so other boats might know their course, avoiding collisions. [111]

The Okoboji Protective Association, or OPA, which had been pushing the legislature for a speed limit on the lakes since Urvin Meyerdirk's death, was pleased with the new regulations. Former Judge Charles S. Bradshaw, the governor's friend and current OPA president, couldn't help but suggest the legislature held some responsibility for the accident. He recalled how the General Assembly failed or refused to pass legislation regulating the speed of motorboats until after there was a second fatal accident. "Now that the horse is out of the barn, we can close the doors," he mocked. [112] Iowa's outboard motorboat associations were against the regulations, and *The Des Moines Register* suggested the speed limit would merely handicap Iowa's water resorts and would have a negligible safety effect.

The day after the governor left Spirit Lake, Welty appeared before the regular meeting of the Dickinson County Board of Supervisors with Assistant State's Attorney Carl J. Stephens. Welty asked to be relieved of the accident investigation because he had been charged with partisanship. He recommended the board allow Stephens to select a special prosecutor to proceed with the case. The board agreed, and by week's end Stephens recommended John "Jake" Hess of Council Bluffs, Iowa, a veteran Pottawattamie County attorney and one of the most able prosecutors in the state.

The board hired Hess, and for the next three weeks he, Welty, and state agents Mead and Elmer C. McPherson reinterviewed the witnesses who had appeared in court. They expanded their investigation to include boat owners, pilots, lakefront concessionaires, state officials and anyone else who might have information that would help in the investigation. Then, for six days in late August, Hess and Welty presented more than 32 witnesses to

---

[111] Ibid.
[112] "THE WAY OF A MAN WITH THE LAW," *Times-Republican (Marshalltown, Iowa)*, Wednesday, July 31, 1929: 4

The Death Boat

the grand jury empaneled by Judge James DeLand at Spirit Lake.

On August 29, the grand jury handed down five indictments. They charged the pilots Yarns, Long and Alexander with manslaughter and John and Milo Hartman with conspiracy to destroy another person's business. DeLand issued warrants for their arrest and released the men on $2,500 bonds. They were to be tried in the next term of court.

Judge Fred C. Lovrien, a four-term state representative, inherited the cases against Yarns and the other pilots and the owners of *Zipper* when Governor Hammill appointed him to replace Judge Daniel F. Coyle. Judge Coyle had resigned to return to private practice after serving 23 years on the bench of the 14th District.

Lovrien took the bench Monday, September 2, and spent his first three weeks hearing cases in Estherville. On Monday, September 23, he opened court in Spirit Lake. By then, Hess and Welty had decided to try the three pilots and the Hartmans separately. When Hess arrived in Spirit Lake, Friday, September 27, the judge heard defense motions to quash the indictments against the pilots, which he overruled. They were arraigned and pleaded not guilty. He scheduled Yarns to be tried the following week. The indictments of Long, Alexander and the Hartmans' were continued until the next term.

Welty filed a motion for a change of venue, hoping to move the trial out of Dickinson County. Sympathy for Yarns had been growing around the Lakes, and many questioned Welty's theory that Yarns might have caused the accident. The *Omaha World-Herald* reflected the feelings of many in the county when it scoffed that "one navigator with a large number of passengers in his own craft deliberately rammed the other boat is a theory of the accident too extreme to be very seriously considered."[113]

Judge Lovrien overruled the motion, and Tuesday morning Yarns stood up in open court and said he was ready to stand trial. By noon Wednesday, a jury of 11 men and one woman was chosen, and the trial began. Hess summarized the case for the state from the manslaughter indictment that

---

[113] "GET THE TRUTH AT OKOBOJI," *Omaha World Herald*, Thursday, August 1, 1929: 10

said Yarns had "willfully, feloniously, wantonly, recklessly, negligently, unlawfully and with reckless indifference to the safety and lives of others" caused the death of Luella Adams.[114]

Addressing the court for the defense was former Judge Coyle, who had been summoned to assist Harry Narey and Walter Bedell. He told Judge Lovrien the indictments and charges were inappropriate and pleaded with the judge to decide the matter from the bench. Hess countered that the former judge was "just talking for effect."[115] Judge Lovrien thought about it overnight, then ruled the trial would proceed.

With the broken piece of *Miss Thriller* again on display, Hess began calling witnesses, starting with the schoolboys Kenneth Darlington and Roy Barnes. He then called Mary Cummings, Helga Hansen, Guy Hedrick and Jap Alexander. They reviewed descriptions of the boats, the route of the trip and the circumstances of the accident. None of *Miss Thriller's* passengers had seen *Zipper* or its headlight until the boat was within approximately 200 feet of *Miss Thriller*.

After those aboard the launch had finished testifying, Hess called Frank Hopkins, the pilot of *Reliance*. Hopkins told the court he arrived at the scene of the accident within three minutes of when he and his passengers heard the crash and the screaming passengers. *Miss Thriller* was already gone and he picked up all the people he could find in the water.

On Friday, Hess called all six adult passengers who had been aboard *Zipper*. The story of what happened on the launch began to unfold with their testimony. Yarns, they said, had moved right, trying to increase the separation between the boats. He tried to alert the passengers and pilots on *Miss Thriller* with his headlight and turned behind *Miss Thriller* moments before the crash trying to avoid the boat. All testified that Yarns provided them with life preservers after the impact and tried to reassure and calm the passengers as he held Philip Schneider out of the water until rescuers arrived.

After the passengers had finished their stories, all of the accident survivors, except Lucille Patterson, who was too ill to make the trip from Des Moines,

---

[114] Manslaughter Indictment, State of Iowa vs. Harold Yarnes [*sic*]
[115] "Jury Drawn for Harold Yarnes [*sic*] Trial," *The Milford Mail*, Thursday, October 3, 1929: 1

The Death Boat

had testified. Lastly, Hess called Bert O'Farrell, owner and operator of the launch *Iona*, and Roy Roff, pilot of the *Queen*. Both testified to what Inspector Thompson had said earlier at the coroner's inquest: that it was the custom among pilots on Lake Okoboji to keep 100 feet from one another's boats.

The state's case finished, Judge Lovrien adjourned for the weekend. Bedell told reporters that on Monday he would ask the judge to dismiss the charge of manslaughter against Yarns. The state, he said, hadn't presented any evidence a crime had been committed.

When court opened Monday afternoon, Bedell presented his motion. The attorneys argued back and forth for almost three hours before Judge Lovrien sustained the motion, dismissing the charges. In doing so, Lovrien reviewed the testimony given by the passengers aboard *Zipper*. He said Yarns' use of the headlight to get the attention of *Miss Thriller* showed his good intentions, not only to control his own launch but also to warn the other boat of his exact presence. His gradual bearing to the right to increase the distance between the two launches as *Miss Thriller* approached, when he had every reason to suspect she was returning to Arnolds Park and would not cross his path, appeared to be prudent. When, for some unknown reason, *Miss Thriller* suddenly turned left and directly across his path, Yarns stopped his engine and turned sharply left to avoid what seemed to be an inevitable collision.

"What should the defendant have done he did not do, or what did he do that he should not have done" the judge asked. "It seems to me that he used the best judgment that he could have used"[116] Lovrien continued that it appeared the cause of the disaster was the sudden change of the course by *Miss Thriller*. "This defendant [is] absolutely free from even the slightest degree of negligence. And I want to say further that the whole conduct of the defendant tends to show that he was not unmindful of the safety of his passengers or of the passengers upon the other boat. In fact the whole record is a showing of the good intentions on the part of the defendant

---

[116] "Judge Lovrien Tells Jury to Free H. Yarnes [*sic*]," *The Spencer Reporter*, Wednesday, October 16, 1929: 8

towards all the people upon the water."[117]

Then, Judge Lovrien took another step, one that might seem unnecessary after having dismissed the manslaughter charge. Addressing the court, the judge said, "It becomes my duty to direct the jury to bring in a verdict for the defendant and I so direct."[118] The jury quickly returned a verdict of not guilty and Lovrien dismissed the case. Yarns never took the stand.

In a telephone interview the next day, Welty told a reporter for *The Spencer News-Herald*, "The rest of the defendants will be taken in order at the next term of court."[119] What he knew and did not say, however, was that having failed to convict Yarns, who had struck *Miss Thriller,* he had little chance of convicting Long and Alexander who appeared to be the victims of the accident.

Before the November term of court, Welty asked the Dickinson County Board of Supervisors whether he should go to the expense of a trial against the other pilots. Board members said they didn't feel qualified to judge based on the merits of the cases and left the decision to Welty. Welty decided to pursue the conspiracy charges against John and Milo Hartman and try pilots Long and Alexander later.

The last Monday of November, Welty brought John and Milo Hartman before Judge Fred C. Davidson. They pleaded not guilty and requested separate trials. The court agreed and assigned Milo to be tried first, in December.

John and Milo Hartman had been charged with conspiracy to destroy the property and business of Frank Long and Jasper Alexander, owners of *Miss Thriller*, under Section 13162 of the 1927 Code of Iowa. It read, "If any two or more persons conspire or confederate together with the fraudulent or malicious intent wrongfully to injure the person, character, business, property, or rights in property of another they are guilty of a conspiracy."[120] The law had its roots in the labor unrest from the turn of the century and

---

[117] "Lake Boat Probe Closes," *The Milford Mail*, Thursday, October 10, 1929: 5
[118] "Judge Lovrien Tells Jury to Free H. Yarnes [sic]," *The Spencer Reporter*, Wednesday, October 16, 1929: 1
[119] "Yarnes [sic] Freed When Case Is Dismissed by Judge; To Try Others Later," *The Spencer News-Herald*, Thursday, October 10, 1929: 9
[120] IOWA CODE Sec. 13162 (1927)

was intended to offer businesses a measure of protection from union picketing and employee strikes.

In court, Milo and his attorneys requested a change in venue, arguing that he couldn't get a fair trial in Dickinson County. Certainly the Hartmans had their supporters, business associates, and friends, but many in the county didn't like John Hartman's hard-nosed business practices. Some resented his power, others were envious of his success and many saw Long and Alexander as victims in the passenger-boat business rivalry. Judge Davidson rejected the change-of-venue motion, and Milo's trial began December 9.

The trial represented an extension of the July dock warfare, now to be recorded in District Court transcripts and punctuated by frequent outbursts from the attorneys. The state's witnesses testified to the name-calling and the intimidation of passengers aboard *Miss Thriller*, some of whom walked off the docks under the withering insults. Milo, they testified, shouted at ticket buyers that *Miss Thriller* had been dug up from the bottom of the St. Lawrence River and was not fit to ride in. "If it was not for the fact that the boat inspector is a relative of one of the operators it would not be licensed,"[121] he had told them. He often displayed his photograph of the boat sunk at her dock as a warning of what could happen. Witnesses testified he shouted at the crowds along the beach with his megaphone that the Hartmans would "put them out of business."[122]

Opening for the defense, Coyle, the former judge, began with a remark intended to endear himself to the jury, telling them this was "the first time in my life I have made a statement before a jury of both men and women."[123, 124] Then, he called his first witness, Milo Hartman. Milo denied almost every accusation made by the state's witnesses and said he had "too much respect for women"[125] to have made the statements attributed to him. The rest of Coyle's witnesses testified it was Long and Alexander who had

---

[121] Genevieve Long, Notice of Additional Testimony, State of Iowa vs. Milo Hartman, Case File 40360, December 9, 1929.
[122] State v. Hartman, No. 40360, Supreme Court of Iowa, 233 N.W. 533 (Iowa 1930)
[123] MILO HARTMAN TRIAL OPENS, *The Mason City Globe-Gazette*, Tuesday, December 10, 1929: 1
[124] Daniel F. Coyle was elected judge of the 14th District in November of 1906. Women became subject to jury service with the adoption of the 19th Amendment, August 18, 1920.
[125] Milo Hartman Denies Accusations Made At Lake Conspiracy Trial, *Creston (Iowa) News Advertiser*, Thursday, December 12, 1929: 1

damaged the Hartmans' business by tearing down their sign, cutting through their boardwalk's handrails, building an unpermitted dock across their boardwalk, and interfering with the Hartmans' boats while they transported passengers.

In a conspiracy charge, the state needed to prove more than the presence of threats and abuse. Welty needed to prove the Hartmans were colluding to damage Long and Alexander's operation. Welty didn't have any direct evidence of a conspiracy, but he skillfully weaved together his witnesses' testimony into a convincing argument that John and Milo Hartman had worked together to put Long and Alexander out of business.

Attorney Narey flatly rejected a conspiracy and tried to undermine Welty's argument in cross-examination. He asked witnesses whether John was on the docks when Milo said the Hartmans would put Long and Alexander out of business, and did Milo hear John taunting *Miss Thriller's* passengers by saying, "No one but whores and bootleggers patronized that tramp boat line?"[126]

Many newspapers had printed transcripts of the coroner's inquest and quoted witnesses and lawyers during the second-degree and manslaughter trials, but the graphic language now prompted most to spurn printing witness testimony. Instead, newspapers tended to cover this trail by listing jury members and witnesses, and by summarizing arguments and what was known of the incident.

The trial lasted exactly one week. The jury of six men and six women ruled unanimously. Milo, they said, was guilty.

Coyle, Narey and Bedell filed a motion for a new trial the next day. They claimed the verdict was the result of passion and prejudice, and that the defendant did not receive a fair trial. The motion was argued at length Wednesday, December 18, and Judge Davidson eventually overruled the motion. He sentenced Milo to be confined to hard labor at the state penitentiary at Fort Madison, Iowa, for a term not exceeding three years. It was the only sentence provided by law. Davidson gave the defense 10 days to appeal to the Iowa Supreme Court, which it did, and released Milo on

---

[126] State v. Hartman, No. 40360, Supreme Court of Iowa, 233 N.W. 533 (Iowa 1930)

The Death Boat

appeal bond until the Iowa Supreme Court heard his case.

The conviction had nothing to do with the boating accident, but the public and some newspapers saw it otherwise. "Hartman didn't get any more than was coming to him, many seem to think not enough," wrote *The Estherville Enterprise*.[127] The *Emmetsburg (Iowa) Reporter* agreed, "The conviction of Milo Hartman for his participation in the accident which caused the death of nine people in a boat collision should serve as a lesson to all those who act in reckless disregard of others' lives under dangerous circumstances."[128]

Earl Peck, son of the amusement park owner and its manager, defended his friend in a letter to *The Spencer News-Herald*. The conviction "had nothing to do with the responsibility for the boat accident," he wrote.[129] Long and Alexander were perceived as underdogs, and that influenced the jury's decision. He noted that not a single passenger aboard the Hartmans' launch was lost or injured.

Frank Long took offense to Peck's implications and responded in a letter to the *Spirit Lake Beacon*, which had reprinted Peck's letter, defending his character and actions the night of the accident. The Hartmans were guilty of a conspiracy that had been going on for five years, he said. The Eagle Boat Line operators "bragged daily that they had put three previous owners of *Miss Thriller* on the rocks and that they would put us there [too]."[130]

By the time John Hartman was brought to trial in September 1930, the court agreed he couldn't get a fair trial in Spirit Lake. Judge Lovrien moved the trial to Pocahontas, Iowa, 70 miles away. Jury selection began Friday morning, September 12, and by Saturday afternoon a jury of 10 farmers, a grain dealer and a housewife was empaneled. The state began its case that afternoon.

The testimony was essentially a repeat of Milo's trial. The state's contention was that John Hartman wouldn't tolerate competition on the lake and all

---

[127] "MILO HARTMAN GETS THREE YEARS IN BOAT DISASTER," *The Estherville Enterprise*, Wednesday, December 25, 1929: 1
[128] "Hartman Conviction A Good Lesson," *Palo Alto (Iowa) Reporter*, Thursday, December 25, 1929: 2
[129] "HARTMANS NOT ALL TO BLAME," *The Spencer News-Herald*, Thursday, January 9, 1930: 2
[130] "Who Was To Blame," *Spirit Lake Beacon*, Thursday, January 23, 1930: 4

rival boat lines would be put out of business. Eight witnesses substantiated the testimony of both Long and Alexander that the Hartmans had used vile, obscene and abusive language toward them in the presence of prospective customers and that Milo Hartman shouted warnings to those on shore, often with a megaphone, not to ride on *Miss Thriller*.

Coyle, Narey and Bedell tried to counter that *Miss Thriller's* operators were the aggressors in the dock warfare. Long and Alexander had cut through Hartman's handrail, pulled down his advertising signs and built a dock across his boardwalk, all under the cover of early morning darkness. The attorneys pointed out that Long and Alexander were operating their business on the lakefront to which John Hartman had leased exclusive rights and that they were conducting business from city property after the mayor had told them to stop. Finally, Long and Alexander were operating without a permit from the state conservation board as required by law.

As before, heated arguments and shouting were common in the courtroom, what *The Spencer News-Herald* called "fireworks,"[131] as the state and defense counsels objected to each other's efforts to disparage witnesses and their testimony.

Tuesday, after the state rested its case, Coyle moved for a directed verdict for the defendant. He told the court that the state had presented only weak, circumstantial evidence that John conspired with Milo to run Long and Alexander out of business. After a day and a half of arguments, Judge Lovrien sustained the motion and directed a verdict for the defendant. Lovrien, in support of freeing John, said the state had to prove a concerted understanding between father and son to put the rival boat line out of business. "This," the judge said, "the state failed to show."[132]

Welty appealed Judge Lovrien's decision to the Iowa Supreme Court. In March 1932, the high court dismissed his appeal. Welty had prosecuted three trials but ultimately failed to hold anyone accountable for the deaths of the nine passengers.

---

[131] "Fireworks Mark Hartman Trial," *The Spencer News-Herald,* Thursday, September 18, 1930: 1

[132] "Directed Verdict by Judge Acquits John Hartman of Conspiracy with Son Milo," *Pocahontas (Iowa) Democrat,* Thursday, September 18, 1930: 1

Milo Hartman had appealed his conviction to the Iowa Supreme Court, and in November 1930, the court upheld his conviction. "The evidence shows a co-operation and concerted conduct between the father and the son to harm...the business of Long and Alexander. No other conclusion can be reached from the testimony,"[133] wrote Chief Justice Elma Albert.

Milo was still out on appeal bond when, in May 1931, Narey convinced the Iowa Supreme Court to rehear the appeal. The following November, the justices reversed Milo's conviction. This time, the high court took a different view of the evidence. Long and Alexander "were the aggressors and instigated the warfare by building the dock and tearing down the property of the Hartmans. Considering the character of the evidence under consideration, the length of time it was before the jury and all the other facts and circumstances in the case, we are constrained to hold the defendant did not receive a fair trial, and the cause must be, and is reversed," wrote Justice John Grimm,[134] (no relation to the Dickinson County coroner). Milo was never confined to the state penitentiary at Fort Madison.

Welty never brought pilots Long and Alexander to trial. Their manslaughter charges dragged on with continuances for another year, then Welty dismissed the charges in November 1932, citing insufficient evidence. Other legal action as the result of the fatal boating accident would linger in the courts for 11 more months but attempts to hold someone responsible for the death of the nine passengers had ended.

---

[133] State v. Hartman, No. 40360, Supreme Court of Iowa, 233 N.W. 533 (Iowa 1930)
[134] State v. Hartman, No. 40360, Supreme Court of Iowa, 239 N.W. 107 (Iowa 1931)

Chapter Eleven

The Recovery of *Miss Thriller*

The first attempts to recover *Miss Thriller* began the morning of Monday, July 29, 1929, as soon as the fleet of rowboats dragging for bodies moved off the site where she sank. Officials were desperate to recover the boat because they believed as many as three bodies could be trapped in the hull.

Pilot Roy Roff steamed the *Queen* out to the scene of the accident and began circling the oil slick while volunteers dragged grappling hooks over the side of the steamer trying to snag the launch 96 feet below. On an early pass, the hooks caught in the wooden seats, tearing them away. The boards came to the surface with such force that they popped six feet out of the water. Twice, the men hooked the boat with a good hold. With almost 25 men on the line stretched down the center of the *Queen*, they pulled against *Miss Thriller*. Once, they seemed to raise the boat 25 feet, but both times the line snapped under the weight of the four-ton launch, and she settled back to the bottom. With no hold on the boat at dark, they came off the water. By the time the *Queen* reached shore, Coroner P. G. Grimm had determined that all the missing had been accounted for, and plans to hire a deep-sea diver to recover the wreck, authorized in a telegram from the governor, were abandoned.

Efforts to recover *Miss Thriller* resumed Tuesday morning. No longer a search for bodies, officials wanted the hull for whatever clues it might provide about the cause of the accident. Landmarks on shore helped pilot Roff return to the launch, and she was quickly hooked. Reinforced with

The Death Boat

heavier rope and a windlass to do the pulling, the *Queen*'s full weight was put on the line only to have the two-inch-thick steel anchor arm straighten and pull out of the boat. Wednesday's efforts were delayed until steel cable and heavier hooks were brought to the lake, but they still were not able to raise the launch. By week's end, with the coroner's inquest concluded and second-degree murder charges dropped, it no longer seemed necessary to recover the launch. Attempts to raise *Miss Thriller* were abandoned.

It appeared as if she would remain on the bottom forever, but that changed in late October. After a trip to Chicago where he had been shopping for boats, Frank Long announced he was going to recover *Miss Thriller*. Long apparently still had an arrangement with Dick Davis to purchase the launch. He said her engines would be salvaged and installed on two new boats he would run on West Lake Okoboji the next season. He told reporters he planned to raise the launch through the ice after the lake had frozen firm enough to support the work.

The lake froze over November 29, and markers were placed on the ice over the wreck. Weather conditions, and perhaps financial difficulties, delayed recovery efforts until the third week of February 1930. By then, shifting ice had rendered the markers useless, and new efforts to locate the wreck were necessary. A crew of men working under the direction of Harry Tennant, who had directed the efforts to recover the bodies after the accident, began chopping holes in the ice and probing the bottom with coupled lengths of gas pipe. The work was slow in the bitter cold. It took almost two weeks to locate *Miss Thriller*, and by then Davis had sold *Miss Thriller* where she lay. The buyers were Milford businessman and well-digger Arthur "Art" Clark, the younger brother of her former owner Let Clark, and her former pilot Pete Eckman.

Tennant's soundings revealed *Miss Thriller* had settled in the lake at an angle, her stern in the mud and her bow off the bottom. Tennant's men cut a large hole in the ice above the wreck and sank a framework of iron pipes around the hull. A loop of heavy chain was wrapped around the framework and lowered to the lake bottom. The pipes were removed, and a windlass on the ice cinched the loop tight around the boat so lifting could begin.

It was late in the season, and the ice cover wouldn't remain intact much longer, so the men worked day and night. They used lamplight and the headlights of cars parked on the ice to work after dark. Drawing the launch to the surface with the windlass, they had raised the boat about 30 to 35 feet when, about 6 p.m. Sunday, March 9, she slipped out of the chain and back to the bottom. Five days later, warming weather caused the ice on the lake to break apart, making further work impossible. Attempts to recover *Miss Thriller* were abandoned again.

The following summer, *Miss Thriller's* new owners, Clark and Eckman, still intending to salvage her engines, began searching for a deep-sea diver to raise their boat from the lake bottom. In the 1930s, hardhat divers generally limited their diving to about 30 feet of water. Most considered deeper dives too dangerous; they would be working in the dark and risked developing the bends, which at *Miss Thriller's* depth could be life-threatening. The first three divers Clark and Eckman contacted refused to consider the recovery, but in June they found a tough, seasoned professional, Captain Horace Herbert Thompson of Duluth, Minnesota.

Thompson grew up along the Great Lakes. Born in 1873, at age 16 he was crewing aboard his father's tugboat, and at 20 he had a pilot's license to run steamships between Duluth, Chicago, and Buffalo, New York. In 1898, after a dynamite explosion killed a hardhat diver working in the Duluth Ship Canal, he bought the damaged gear, had it refurbished, and began hiring himself out as a submarine diver.

The self-taught diver found work immediately in underwater construction, ship repair, and wreck recovery. He laid gas and water lines under the Duluth Ship Canal and worked on piers in Lake Superior, locks on the Mississippi River, and a dam in New Mexico. By 1930, Thompson was a veteran of underwater construction, wreck salvaging, and the dangerous work of diving on broken ships among their entangling cables, crumpled structures, and splintered decks. He had survived life-threatening accidents and had been hardened by the recovery of bodies. Most important to Clark and Eckman, Thompson was willing to travel to West Lake Okoboji and attempt to recover *Miss Thriller*.

The evening of Monday, June 30, 1930, Thompson arrived at Okoboji with his diving equipment: a canvas suit and its 55-pound helmet, a 60-pound lead-weighted diving vest, a pair of brass boots that weighed 18 pounds each, and a hand-pumped air compressor. With him was his middle son,

John Thompson, who manned the tethering line and rubber hose that supplied air to the suit. He would direct the compressor's operation.

Early the next morning, Albert "Bert" O'Farrell, a passenger-boat owner and operator and Dickinson County deputy sheriff, took Thompson to the wreck site aboard his motor launch, *Iona*. It takes 20 minutes to gear up for a hardhat dive, but it may have taken Thompson longer on the small launch crowded with volunteers, salvaging equipment and the air compressor. Burdened by the 150-pound suit, Thompson pulled himself onto *Iona*'s gunwales, swung himself onto a ladder lashed to the side of the boat with chain, climbed down to the last rung, looped a line anchored near the launch into the crook of his arm, and let go. Sinking into the deep water as quickly as John could feed out the hose and line, Captain H.H. Thompson became the first person to dive West Lake Okoboji.

Thompson dropped to the bottom of the lake, 35 feet deeper than he'd ever been in his life, and sank into two feet of thick muck. He was shrouded in total darkness, and cold water squeezed his suit against his body. Thompson was immersed in the clearest water in the lake. A lamp's beam could have pierced 80 feet into the darkness, but he had no light, and sunlight never reaches below 66 feet in West Lake Okoboji.

He also had dropped below the thermocline, the seam between the waters near the surface that warm and cool with the seasons and the deep waters that remain about 54 degrees year-round. The seam was so sharp he could feel it cross his body as he passed through. With no more protection from the cold than his street clothes inside the canvas suit, he began his search in the darkness for *Miss Thriller*.

He should have been within feet of the boat, but with nothing but open bottom for a half-mile in every direction but one, which way should he go? Balancing himself with his outstretched arms, he dragged a weighted boot through the mud with each labored step. Thompson left no record of what search pattern he used or whether it was experience, instinct, or perhaps mere good luck that guided his steps, but he located the launch. He then surveyed every inch of the boat with his hands. His examination told him she was bottom up, turned over during the spring attempt to bring her to the surface. Her engine-heavy stern was embedded in the muddy bottom. Thompson attached a line to the hull to aid in his return and ascended to the surface. He had been on the bottom of the lake more than three hours.

Warmed and recovered, Thompson made a second dive Tuesday afternoon. He followed the line directly down to *Miss Thriller*. He felt his way along the hull until he reached the transom. Working from his knees in the dark, cold water, he dug through the mud by hand, uncovered her propellers, wrapped a chain around the drive shafts, and hooked it to a 5/8-inch steel cable he had brought down with him from the deck of the *Queen*. Once he was out of the water, the steamer began pulling on *Miss Thriller*. The *Queen* pitched badly to one side under the strain, and before *Miss Thriller* could be pulled from the mud, the cable snapped. Either it was cut by the chains or pulled apart by the strain. With the hold on the boat lost and too late for another dive, the day's work ended.

It was noon Wednesday before Thompson would dive again. By then, a plan had been devised to use a double-pull to raise *Miss Thriller*. Thompson would descend to the launch, wrap a chain around the entire stern of the boat and secure a large pulley to the chain. He then would feed a cable from a windlass on the *Queen*'s deck through the pulley and back to the surface, where it would be secured to a second windlass aboard the steamer. The crewmen aboard the *Queen* would be able to pull with either or both windlasses with no chance of cutting the cable, and pilot Roff could apply all of the steamer's towing power in any direction necessary to work *Miss Thriller* free from the mud.

During another long dive, Thompson dug his way under the hull, pulled the chain around the boat, secured a pulley block to the chain, and threaded a cable from the *Queen* through the sheave and back to the surface. With *Miss Thriller* securely fastened to the *Queen* and Thompson out of the water, the steamer pulled on the wreck, moving back and forth above the boat as crewmen pulled with the winches until the mucky bottom finally gave way. *Miss Thriller* was winched out of the mud, raised off the bottom, and towed toward Brown's Bay. Her bow dragged across the sand when she reached shallow water.

The towing continued late into the evening. The steamer pulled the boat as close to Terrace Park Beach as her bottom would allow, and from there she would have to be pulled on shore from the beach.

Thursday was a disappointing day for the crowd along the shore who had come to see *Miss Thriller* breach the lake's surface. For two days, small groups of people watched the *Iona* and *Queen* working over the site of the wreck, and they followed the steamer as she crossed the lake into Brown's Bay. Now near shore where they could easily see the work, people flocked to the beach to watch the deep-sea diver and see the boat come ashore.

Captain Thompson, on the deck of *Iona,* prepares to dive for *Miss Thriller.* Standing next to him is his son John Thompson. The two men on the right are Pete Eckman, standing behind John Thompson, and Art Clark.

Courtesy of the Iowa Great Lakes Maritime Museum

Clark and Eckman sent for one of the largest tractors in the area, an Aultman & Taylor Model 30-60 owned by Perry Wilson of Milford. It took hours to lumber the 12-ton gasoline tractor with its seven-and-a-half-foot steel rear wheels to the lake. The tractor was backed as near the water as the sand would support.

Thompson, working beneath the *Iona* in water shallow enough for him to see, began what became a struggle with chain and cable to find a hold on the boat that would roll it upright rather than draw it nearer shore. With each grip, the tractor would test the pull only to be stopped again and slack added to the line so Thompson could try another arrangement. The work lasted all day as holds slipped or failed to roll the launch. By dusk, such a large crowd had gathered on the beach and was milling about the tractor, cables, and workmen that Chester Tyrrell, the state's lake custodian, deemed the work too dangerous to continue. Efforts were postponed until the next day.

Friday morning, a new hold finally rolled *Miss Thriller* upright. The water above the wreck turned black in what looked like a rolling boil as the shifting mud from her insides mixed with the sand scraped from the bottom when she rolled over. Life preservers, most of their buoyancy soaked out, drifted slowly to the surface from their compartments under the seats. At noon on the Fourth of July, 1930—11 months and eight days after she had sunk—*Miss Thriller* was pulled onto Terrace Park Beach.

Onlookers, many of whom had kept a faithful vigil since she arrived in shallow water Wednesday evening, splashed into the lake to get a closer look. Some climbed onto the hull almost before it broke water while Clark and Eckman tried to keep people away to prevent injuries and souvenir hunting as the powerful tractor drew her up on the beach.

Miss Thriller was a sorry sight, ravaged by the crash and the recovery efforts. Her decking was splintered. Her seats were pulled apart and broken by grappling hooks that also left scars along her deck, sides, and bottom. Deep chain impressions were evident around her stern. Some who had come to the lake to see her recovery were surprised to see she was a white boat with black lettering. A widely published photograph from *The Des Moines Register* at the time of her sinking showed a dark *Miss Thriller* with white lettering above a caption that read "Picture was snapped prior to the crash as it was moored to the pier."[135] Though the caption may have suggested otherwise, the *Register* had used an old photograph.

Controversy began as soon as she broke the surface of the water. Tyrrell, who had been appointed custodian in June, ordered the boat removed from the state's property immediately. He wasn't going to have the state held responsible for any damage caused by scavengers or injuries to curious onlookers. Dan Jeppson, mayor of West Okoboji, issued a contrary order allowing the boat to remain on the city's beach until Monday. An agreement

---

[135] "More Scenes From the Rescue Work After the Okoboji Lake Disaster," *The Des Moines Register,* Tuesday, July 30, 1929: 15

was reached allowing the boat to remain, covered with canvas and under guard to keep souvenir hunters away, until Monday.

The long, deep dives of the recovery took a toll on Captain Thompson. He later would say that recovering *Miss Thriller* was the most difficult feat of his 32 years of diving. The day after she was pulled onto the beach, he had Sheriff George Paulson place a lien on the boat for $900, but it was released Monday to Clark and Eckman when her former owner, Dick Davis, an officer of the Security National Bank in Milford, signed bonds guaranteeing Thompson would be paid.

Miss Thriller is covered with tarps after being pulled onto Terrace Park Beach.
Courtesy of the Iowa Great Lakes Maritime Museum

Before Thompson left the Lakes, he allowed several men and a woman, Cecelia Addy, to don his diving suit and walk about on the lake bottom from the beach at Arnolds Park. Addy became the first woman to dive West Lake Okoboji. A farm wife and occasional correspondent for *The Sioux City Journal*, she was born in a sod house in nearby Lakefield, Minnesota, and lived with her husband, Edward Addy, and 9-year-old daughter, Carolyn, in Lake Park, Iowa. Carolyn cried as her mother disappeared underwater, afraid she might not return. Addy was a confident, independent, and daring woman who, when Iowa later required licenses, would become the first woman licensed to drive in Dickinson County.

Clark and Eckman, who claimed to have about $2,600 invested in the boat and its recovery, said the engines appeared to be in perfect condition. They planned to install them in a pair of hydroplanes. They also confirmed rumors that they planned to exhibit the remains of *Miss Thriller* and hoped to have the boat on display by the week's end.

Cecelia Addy in Captain Thompson's diving suit,
Thompson is on the right.
Courtesy of the Addy family

They met with a wall of local resistance. Arnolds Park's mayor and residents were united in refusing to have the tragedy commercialized. They insisted the boat be destroyed as soon as the engines were salvaged. Bert E. Thompson, who was an Arnolds Park businessman, Arnolds Park Savings Bank director and former steamboat captain, told reporters that the people of Arnolds Park "would never permit this lake disaster to be capitalized by the exhibition of this boat."[136] Both amusement parks refused substantial sums for a place to exhibit the launch, and some residents wrote letters to Governor Hammill requesting he forbid the boat's exhibition.

Unable to find a place to exhibit the launch in Arnolds Park, Clark and Eckman set her up on a vacant lot in the Maywood addition just south of town. They put signs along the highway advertising her exhibition and began charging 25 cents to see the boat. At first, hundreds of people paid to see the wreck, but the novelty quickly subsided. Clark and Eckman moved her to Milford and then tried exhibiting her at county fairs. They found little success.

In September, they placed *Miss Thriller* in a tent across the street from the main entrance of the Clay County Fair in Spencer. Fair officials were unhappy about the morbid display, but it was on private property. There was nothing they could do. By November, under constant protest from the

---
[136] "Recovery Of The "Thriller" Recalls Okoboji Tragedy," *Ringsted (Iowa) Dispatch,* Thursday, July 10, 1930: 1

public and editors across the state who said they were "commercializing death"[137] and making a "sideshow of the wreck"[138] while no one had yet been punished for the death of her passengers, Clark and Eckman abandoned efforts to make money displaying the boat. They discarded *Miss Thriller* on a junk pile along a side street in Milford.

---

[137] "Commercializing Death," *The Jefferson (Iowa) Bee,* Wednesday, November 5, 1930: 2
[138] Ibid.

Chapter Twelve

Epilogue

The state's response to the accident changed boating in Iowa forever. Chairman W.E.G. Saunders of the state conservation board made good his words from the day he walked out of Yarns' second-degree murder hearing. In early October, he initiated a series of public hearings to draft boating regulations for Iowa lakes. The following February, the board adopted rules that set the speed limit for boats at 15 miles an hour during daylight hours and 10 miles an hour at night. Speedboats capable of more than 20 miles an hour were barred from the water from sunset to sunrise. Choosing to use the word "speedboats" allowed the steamboats to operate at night again.

For the first time, all boats in the state were required to carry a life preserver for each person aboard, have air chambers of sufficient capacity to sustain the boat when full of water and a full complement of passengers and crew on board, have a fire extinguisher and display colored lights on the bow at night, red showing to the port, green showing starboard. They also were required to display an elevated white light at the rear that could be seen from all directions. Such lighting would reveal a boat's location and direction of travel to other boaters in the dark.

In April 1930, the board visited Arnolds Park. It ordered C.P. Benit, and Dr. A.L. Peck to clear the lakefront of their remaining buildings and announced that a 10-foot-wide boardwalk would be laid the full length of the beach. Speedboat operators could lease dock space extending from the state-owned boardwalk for one-third of the income they generated. The board also said a uniformed officer would be assigned to the lakefront to enforce the new boating regulations.

In June, the board let a contract to build a public pier at the end of Lake Street. It would be an 80-foot-wide circular structure extending 100 feet into the lake. It was designed to allow cars to drive to the end, make a turn and return.

Construction began in early July and was well underway when Peck went to court seeking an injunction preventing the state from building the pier. At 80 feet, it was wider than the Lake Street access, therefore extending in front of Peck's property and interfering, he claimed, with his property rights. Work was suspended as the case was argued before Judge Fred C. Lovrien. The judge agreed with the state that the lake was state property and the pier could be built any way the state deemed proper. Construction resumed. In September, Peck filed a lawsuit against the construction company building the pier. Judge Fred C. Davidson dismissed the lawsuit. Peck appealed his cases to the Iowa Supreme Court. In October 1932, months after the pier had been completed and John Hartman and Lo Gipner had been operating passenger launches from the state's boardwalk at the new price of $200 a year, the Supreme Court ruled for the state. Except for the occasional minor arrest for violating the new boating regulations, the Arnolds Park lakefront was quiet again.

In spring 1930, Captain William Ewart Gladstone Saunders, a Spanish-American War veteran and former three-term state legislator, ran in the Republican primary for secretary of state. Conservation groups savagely attacked him throughout the campaign. They accused him of being ultimately responsible for the accident because he had given Long and Alexander permission to build their dock. Saunders, who had discussed the matter with the other board members before giving the boatmen permission, defended his action, saying he saw no reason to allow a monopoly for the passenger-launch business at Arnolds Park.

The criticism might have cost him the election. In a four-man race, he was a close second, but when none of the candidates received the required 35 percent of the votes in the primary, the nomination shifted to the state convention. The delegates selected Gilbert C. Greenwalt of Des Moines, who went on to win in the November general election. Saunders served out his term on the board, retired, and moved to California.

Car traffic snuffed out the great steamboat era on West Lake Okoboji. Hard-surfaced roads reached all of the popular attractions and almost every family now owned a car. Steamboat pilots Alphonso and Elmer Henderson, who had built, owned, and operated many of the larger steamers, left the Lakes. Alphonso migrated west to Flathead Lake, Montana, where he built and operated steamboats into the 1940s. Elmer returned to his native Illinois, and settled in Brookport. He piloted tugboats on the Ohio River for almost 15 years. His funeral service announcement honored him with the title "Retired Riverman."[139]

One by one, the last of the steamboats disappeared from Lake Okoboji. A month after *Miss Thriller* sank, the *Des Moines* was destroyed by a fire of unknown origin while moored at her dock at Arnolds Park. The *Sioux City* carried her last passengers in 1937 or 1938. In 1942, she was cut apart in a war-effort scrap metal drive. The *Queen* left West Lake Okoboji in 1973. She was pulled out of the water at Terrace Park Beach, loaded onto a large truck and hauled away to become an attraction at a soon-to-open amusement park in Altoona, Iowa.

John Hafer continued building what he proudly called yard-built boats, as opposed to factory-made boats, in Spirit Lake until his death in 1957. The Hafer Boat Works passed to his son, who oversaw the declining interest in Hafer Crafts as wooden boats fell out of fashion. The boatworks closed in 1968.

Charles Parker got off to a rough start in the fruit orchard business. The Sacramento Suburban Fruit Lands Co. swindled Parker by selling him overpriced land unsuitable for orchard production. He sued the company and recovered most of his original investment. Parker and his family went on to become successful fruit farmers in Rio Linda, California.

Before she was an aviatrix, Muriel Hanford, who had entertained the crowds with her biplane the day of the accident, was a vaudeville star. In 1913, she was a Peacock Girl in the "Ziegfeld Follies," preforming in a flamboyant costume of fluffy feathers and peacock plumes. Later, she

---

[139] Massac County, Illinois, funeral home records, Vol. II, 1937-1938

became famous for singing classical and popular songs, and making elaborate costume changes on stage behind a screen that left exposed what one reviewer described as a "dangerous pair of shoulders."[140] She left the stage briefly during World War I to drive ambulances in London and serve meals to British soldiers known as Tommies. She returned as the "Peacock Girl of Vaudeville,"[141] and played the RKO and Orpheum circuits, the Palace Theatre in New York and Drury Lane in London. In 1920, while performing in Sioux City, she met and married Arthur Hanford Jr., her second husband. In 1939, by then Mrs. Muriel Hanford Turnley, she bought the house Wesley Arnold had built in 1882. She remodeled the building into a popular nightclub she called The Peacock Inn. She sold The Peacock in 1946 and moved to Fort Lauderdale, Florida, in 1953, opening Muriel's Jade House. She died in August 1965 from complications following an appendectomy. Her former nightclub, Wesley Arnold's 1882 house, was torn down in 1977.

Jap Alexander continued driving pleasure boats from Arnolds Park during the summers. In 1937, he built Alexander's 66 Service Station, which also served as a paint store, one block north of the bridge at Okoboji. He owned and operated the station for 32 years. He was the first commander of the Arnolds Park American Legion Post 654, which later merged with Milford Post 384. Alexander died Aug. 1, 1969. He was 76 years old.

Frank Long left the Lakes. He moved his family to Braham, Minnesota, in 1937, and then to Park Rapids, Minnesota, in 1939, where he farmed until he entered World War II. After the war, he became a maritime engineer. He served as the chief engineer aboard the motor ship *M.S. Coastal Glacier*, which sailed between Ketchikan, Alaska, and Seattle, Washington, until his death in 1949 from a shipboard accident. He was 62.

Attorneys Kenneth Welty, Harry Narey and Walter Bedell spent their careers practicing law in Spirit Lake. Narey, who had taken his son Peter for a ride on *Miss Thriller* during the dock war of 1929, never thought the boat was seaworthy. He was convinced it never should have been allowed to operate on Iowa waters. County Attorney Welty, who was married to

---

[140] "[The] Palace, Chicago," *Variety (magazine)*, Friday, March 14, 1919: 17
[141] "In Dark Hours His 'Peacock Girl' Fought for Him, But Now-," *The Philadelphia (PA) Inquirer*, June 4, 1933, Magazine Section: 3

Narey's stenographer, lost the office of county attorney to Angus Macdonald in November 1932. After a recount confirmed the race ended in a tie, the Dickinson County Board of Supervisors placed both candidates' names, written on identical cards, in a cigar box. Macdonald's name was drawn. Two years later, Welty was re-elected and served as county attorney from 1934 to 1936. He then returned to private practice. Virginia Bedell, Walter Bedell's wife, succeeded Welty in office. She became Iowa's first female county attorney.

Former state Senator Leslie E. Francis and Governor John Hammill, both Republicans, were friends for years. They had served two terms together in the state Senate. After his second term, Francis ran unsuccessfully for the U.S. Senate. He then returned to private practice and opened law offices in Des Moines. The men often attended and sometimes hosted social events in the capital city. But Francis had grown up at the Lakes, and he understood the financial implications of the governor's hastily written boating rules. His open letter to the governor turned out to be prophetic. The speed limit on the lake and the ban on night passenger boating killed the speedboat business at Okoboji. On the Fourth of July in 1929, *Teaser* took in $400, according to John Hartman's banker. The next Fourth of July, she took in only $30. *Teaser* and *Red Devil* left the lake later that summer, reportedly for lakes in South Dakota.

By 1935, John Hartman sold the rest of his boats, ending the Eagle Boat Line, and retired. His wife, Cora, had died in 1931. She didn't live long enough to see the Supreme Court overturn her son's conviction. Hartman later married Mabel Narey, his attorney's sister. Hartman traveled by motorcar and trailer across the country, often wintering in the Los Angeles, California area and returning for summers. He died in January 1955 at 85.

After Hartman sold the Eagle boats, son Milo sold his variety store, the Hartman 5 & 10 Cent Store. He and his wife, Emma, toured the country by car and settled in Long Beach, California. They worked as managers, promoters and concessioners with traveling circuses for the next 20 years. Milo died in September 1958. He was 66.

Captain H.H. Thompson had asked Sheriff George Paulson to attach a lien on *Miss Thriller* for $900 when she was pulled onto Terrace Park Beach in July 1930, but he still struggled to get paid for salvaging the launch. With so many financial arrangements among her former owners, it wasn't clear who owed him for recovering the boat. Thompson filed a lawsuit against all of them—Art Clark, Pete Eckman, Dick Davis, Jap Alexander and Frank Long—for his services. The lawsuit was settled out of court, after a jury had been empaneled, in December 1930. No record tells what happened to the Liberty airplane engines Captain Thompson recovered from the lake. They had replaced the troublesome Fiat engines that arrived in the boat in 1925. What is remembered is that they were the most expensive C.O.D shipment at $5,500 ever carried to Arnolds Park by railcar. The engines were pulled from the boat before she was put on display. For a while, they were stored in front of Wilson Boat Works on East Okoboji, but then they seemed to disappear. They were never installed on any boat launched at the Lakes.

Harold Yarns lived the rest of his life in the shadow of a reputation he didn't deserve. Despite the testimony from the passengers aboard *Zipper* the night of the accident, to this day some are convinced Yarns was responsible for the deaths of the nine passengers on *Miss Thriller*. *The Graettinger (Iowa) Times*, summarizing the incident in 1933, said Yarns was discharged for lack of evidence, but "in the public mind there has never been any question where responsibility for the killings should have been placed."[142]

A few people still believe he got away with murder and tell stories of gallows built on the Dickinson County Courthouse lawn waiting for the jury to come in with a guilty verdict. Others thought his carelessness or inexperience was responsible for the accident. In truth, gallows never were erected, and Yarns was a skilled boatman. For decades, however, the ugly talk about Yarns would resurface after every retelling of the story of the accident.

The spring after the accident, Yarns asked Inspector Thompson to reinstate his pilot's license. Thompson refused. On May 29, 1930, Yarns wrote to Governor Hammill. Having been exonerated, he wrote, it was "only just and fair" that his license should be reissued.[143] Inspector Thompson, he continued, refused to issue him a license without just cause. The governor replied to Yarns, "I have reviewed the record in your case and I am of the

---

[142] "Last Chapter In History Of 'Miss Thriller'," *The Graettinger Times*, Thursday, February 2, 1933: 1
[143] Notarized enclosure, Harold Yarns to Governor John Hammill, May 29, 1930 TS

opinion that your connection to the accident should not be a barrier to your receiving a renewal of your license."[144] But the governor had no power to issue Yarns a pilot's license. He referred the pilot to the state conservation board, which oversaw pilot licenses. On June 2, 1930, four days after Yarns wrote to the governor, Hammill replaced Thompson, appointing Etton R. Deater as the boating inspector at Okoboji. There are no records confirming that Yarns' pilot's license was reinstated.

Yarns seldom talked about the accident and never spoke publicly about it until 1991 when, at age 87, he shared his story with Larry Keltto, managing editor of *The Spirit Lake Beacon*. As Yarns recalled the accident, "there's pain in his face and his eyes," wrote Keltto.[145] Yarns sketched the paths of the two launches as they approached one another and drew *Miss Thriller's* course, a sharp turn across his path, that resulted in the crash. He told Keltto he never understood why *Miss Thriller* would have turned that way and theorized that Long wanted to turn right but "gunned the wrong engine."[146] Yarns said he had done everything he could to avoid the accident.

Yarns spent the rest of his life in Dickinson County. He farmed near Angler's Bay where he grew up operating boats for his father. For 20 years, he was the engineer of the Okoboji Express, a small-gauge railroad ride in the amusement park. He died April 15, 1994, at age 90.

While state officials might have placated the general public with their response to the accident, they did little to comfort the families and friends who were bearing the pain of lost loved ones. Compounding the sorrow, the state failed to hold anyone accountable for the deaths. Parents grieved for lost children, spouses for their partners, siblings for their companions. Adelor Gelino, the father of victim Neal Gelino, sought a legal remedy by suing the boatmen. His case lingered in the courts for two years until Judge Davidson dismissed it. The grief in the Gelino home was so painful it eroded their marriage; in 1937 it ended in divorce. Neal's grave in Spencer's Riverside Cemetery has never been recorded. No stone marks his final resting place.

---

[144] Governor John Hammill to Harold Yarns, June 6, 1930 TS
[145] "The Tragedy of 1929," *Spirit Lake Beacon*, Thursday, September 26, 1991: 39
[146] Ibid.

The Death Boat

Mary Cummings sued the insurance company of her husband, Lloyd, to recover the death indemnity of his life insurance policy. The company claimed *Miss Thriller* wasn't a common carrier within the coverage of the policy. In 1931, the Minnesota Supreme Court ruled it was and that Mary was entitled to the money.[147]

Laura Hintz, the widow of victim Henry Hintz, moved to Sioux Falls, South Dakota, with Neill, her 16-year-old son. She never remarried.

More than two dozen newspapers published the names of the dead following the accident. None correctly identified all nine victims. Pete Eckman and Coroner Grimm did what they could to identify the victims and corrected their list before it was given to reporters at the coroner's inquest, but they might have made mistakes. Reporters had to wire the names or dictate them over telephone lines with intermittent service to editors at their newspapers who might have misread or misheard the names or made wrong assumptions. Names were misspelled and ages were incorrect.

The names Luella, Gelino, Rehnstrom and Koehnk seemed especially difficult to get right. Neal's name was often spelled Neil, and Thomas Christian was at first identified by his father's name, Carl. Lloyd Cummings never was correctly identified. He was identified at first as Harold and later as Floyd. His last name was most often spelled Cummins. For generations when retelling the story, newspaper, book, and magazine writers, gleaning the names from the original newspaper accounts, have repeated the misspelled names, reopening old wounds in the hearts of the victims' parents, siblings and descendants.

A few lucky people chose not to ride *Miss Thriller* the night of the accident. George and Pearl Jacob of Milford left their seats in the middle of the boat. Some say Pearl became too afraid to ride the launch, others say George wanted to wait and ride in the front seats. Pearl kept her ticket to *Miss Thriller* for the rest of her life and never sat in another boat. At least two couples had already decided to wait for the next trip because the front seats had been taken. Others didn't want to take the open seats in the back row,

---

[147] Mary Cummings v. Great American Casualty Co., 235 N.W. 617 (Minn. 1931)

one of which Neal Gelino slipped into as the boat left the dock.

John Hartman had *Zipper* repaired after the accident. She carried passengers on West Lake Okoboji for years under her new name, *Princess*.[148]

Miss Thriller rested on the junk pile in Milford for more than two years. Launched at Alexandria Bay before a large crowd summoned by exciting newspaper headlines and again on West Lake Okoboji by hundreds who had never seen a sea sled, *Miss Thriller*'s name faded from public attention. When newspapers mentioned her at all, they called her the "Death Boat."[149] To residents of the Lakes, she was a constant reminder of the terrible accident and the loss of life in West Lake Okoboji.

John Steinke passed the boat several times each week. Every time he saw it, he was reminded of his son, Arnold. On Tuesday January 24, 1933, Steinke soaked the hollow, rotting hull with five gallons of gasoline and put a match to her. *Miss Thriller* was burned to ashes. The fastest passenger boat in the country drifted away in smoke.

Well, almost all of her. At least one piece of the launch exists today: a six-inch segment of her propeller shaft is on display at the Iowa Great Lakes Maritime Museum in Arnolds Park. There was and might be a second piece of the launch on the bottom of the lake: one of the pair of used Cadillac headlights installed by Long and Alexander that were still burning when she sank. Perhaps the headlight was pulled off by grappling hooks in the days right after the accident or sheared off by the loop of chain used during the attempts to recover her through the ice. Maybe it was dragged from her bow when she was pulled across the bottom to Terrace Park Beach. Whatever the case, when *Miss Thriller* was pulled from the water, the headlight was missing. It might remain on the bottom of West Lake Okoboji forever.

---

[148] "W. Okoboji boat tragedy 50 years ago recalled," *The Des Moines Register,* Saturday, July 28, 1979: 4
[149] "Will Make New Effort To Raise Death Boat," *The Sioux City (Iowa) Journal,* Saturday, February 22, 1930: 2

The Death Boat

Acknowledgements

So many people contributed to this story that it's not possible to list them all, but I want to single out a few people in particular. The book would not exist without the assistance of Kay Wilson of the Dickinson County Clerk of Court's office. She made room for me in crowded office space to study the records and transcripts of the legal cases that followed the accident. Sharon Avery, government records archivist at the State Historical Society of Iowa, provided me with copies of Supreme Court and legislative documents and records and copies of historic newspaper pages, access to Governor John Hammill's correspondence, and answers to what must have seemed an endless string of questions. Cindy Schubert, curator of the Dickinson County Historical Museum, helped me with local history. I also had help from Mary Kennedy, curator of the Iowa Great Lakes Maritime Museum, from the Coast Guard Historian's Office and The State Law Library of Iowa. Dozens of librarians and research assistants, clerks of court, museum curators and cemetery sextons provided copies of book, magazine and newspaper stories and public records, names, dates, biographies and descriptions of local locations that have become part of the story.

Librarian Linda Miller of the Spirit Lake Public Library was my guide through the microfilm and digital records of the Dickinson County newspapers. Attorney Peter Narey, son of attorney Harry Narey, provided copies from his father's brief to the Iowa Supreme Court that persuaded the Court to rehear Milo Hartman's appeal after they had decided the case. Both Linda and Peter died before the book's publication. I am grateful for the time they shared with me.

Michelle Diehl, Jill Callison, Pat Duncan, Randy Hascall and Rosemary McCoy, friends and former colleagues at the *Argus Leader* in Sioux Falls, South Dakota, all contributed to the book. Michelle, a genealogist, helped me uncover many of the names and family connections that enrich the story. Jill, Pat, Randy and Rosemary edited the story, I cannot thank them enough.

I also want to thank the many people at the Iowa Great Lakes who shared their stories about the Lakes and its history. They all contributed in ways large and small to the story.

Made in the USA
Monee, IL
28 September 2020